Western Bankers in China

When China's economic reforms were beginning, there was an expectation in the West that China's financial markets would be opened to Western banks and that China's banks would be reformed along Western lines. Joint ventures between Chinese banks and Western banks, minority shareholding by Western banks and the involvement of Western banking personnel in assisting Chinese banks with their reforms were all seen as evidence of convergence towards Western management norms. This book analyses the role that Western bankers have played in China's economic reforms, focusing on their influence on institutional change and corporate governance. Based on extensive original research, the book shows that while components of Western models of corporate governance have been widely adopted, the motivation for these changes seems to have been legitimacy-seeking by Chinese banks, and that while there has been relatively rapid change in the formal legislative environment, informal organisational practices are changing at a much slower pace. Alliances between Chinese and Western banks are woven with contradictions and power games, and many actors in the Chinese banking sector seek to resist manipulation by their Western counterparts. The financial crisis of 2008 weakened the idea that Western banks are a universally correct model and strengthened China's resolve to keep control of its banking sector and to manage it in a way that suits China's interests, not those of the West.

Jane Nolan is an Associate Professor in Human Resource Management and Organisational Behaviour in the School of Business at the University of Nottingham.

Routledge Contemporary China Series

The Power of Relationalism in China
Leah Zhu

China's Financial Opening: Coalition Politics and Policy Changes
Yu-Wai Vic Li

Urbanization, Regional Development and Governance in China
Jianfa Shen

Midwifery in China
Ngai Fen Cheung and Rosemary Mander

China's Virtual Monopoly of Rare Earth Elements
Economic, Technological and Strategic Implications
Roland Howanietz

China's Regions in an Era of Globalization
Tim Summers

China's Climate-Energy Policy
Domestic and International Impacts
Edited by Akihisa Mori

Western Bankers in China
Institutional Change and Corporate Governance
Jane Nolan

Xinjiang in the Twenty-First Century
Islam, Ethnicity and Resistance
Michael Dillon

China Studies in the Philippines
Intellectual Paths and the Formation of a Field
Edited by Tina S. Clemente and Chih-yu Shih

For more information about this series, please visit: https://www.routledge.com/Routledge-Contemporary-China-Series/book-series/SE0768

Western Bankers in China

Institutional Change and Corporate Governance

Jane Nolan

Routledge
Taylor & Francis Group
LONDON AND NEW YORK

First published 2019
by Routledge
2 Park Square, Milton Park, Abingdon, Oxon OX14 4RN

and by Routledge
52 Vanderbilt Avenue, New York, NY 10017

First issued in paperback 2020

Routledge is an imprint of the Taylor & Francis Group, an informa business

British Library Cataloguing in Publication Data
A catalogue record for this book is available from the British Library

Library of Congress Cataloging in Publication Data
Names: Nolan, Jane, author.
Title: Western bankers in China : institutional change and corporate governance / Jane Nolan.
Description: Abingdon, Oxon ; New York, NY : Routledge, 2019. | Series: Routledge contemporary China series | Includes bibliographical references and index.
Identifiers: LCCN 2018021504| ISBN 9780415584647 (hardback : alk. paper) | ISBN 9780429445712 (ebook : alk. paper)
Subjects: LCSH: Banks and banking–China–Cross-cultural studies. | Banks and banking, Foreign–China–Cross-cultural studies. | Banks and banking, International–China–Cross-cultural studies.
Classification: LCC HG3334 .N65 2019 | DDC 332.10951–dc23
LC record available at https://lccn.loc.gov/2018021504

ISBN 13: 978-0-36-758521-1 (pbk)
ISBN 13: 978-0-415-58464-7 (hbk)

Typeset in Times New Roman
by Taylor & Francis Books

For my parents, Brian and Christine Nolan

Contents

Tables

Acknowledgements

So many people, from so many parts of the world, have supported me over the course of this project. First and foremost, I would like to thank my research participants who contributed so generously with their time and their ideas. Much of what follows emerged from their insights, as much as from mine. Among my many contacts and informants in China, I would especially like to thank Jian Yi and Wan Yingqun.

The research was funded by a Nuffield Foundation New Career Fellowship and I am grateful to the Foundation for the financial assistance they provided. The Department of Sociology at the University of Cambridge and Magdalene College, Cambridge, also provided a stimulating environment during the development of the project. Colleagues at the University of Leicester and the University of Nottingham have also helped me along the way, some offering critical friendship, others just good old-fashioned, alcohol-fuelled friendship.

While all the research presented here is original, parts of some chapters have been adapted and re-worked from journal articles. Part of Chapter 6 originally appeared in 'The influence of western banks on corporate governance in China,' *Asia Pacific Business Review, 16*(3), 417–436 (© 2010 Taylor & Francis; all rights reserved). Part of Chapter 7 originally appeared in 'Good guanxi and bad guanxi: Western bankers and the role of network practices in institutional change in China,' *The International Journal of Human Resource Management, 22*(16), 3357–3372 (© 2011 Taylor & Francis; all rights reserved).

I could not have completed this research without the guidance and intellectual inspiration of my mentor, Professor Malcom Warner, of the Judge Business School, University of Cambridge. He has been with me through all the complications, stresses and rewards that accompany a project like this. I would also like to thank my publisher, Peter Sowden, editor at Routledge, for his advice, and his patience. I owe a particular debt of gratitude to Sue Chadwick and Mark Whyman for their unending good humour and shrewd observations on life in general.

Finally, I would like to thank my parents, Christine Nolan (1940–2011) and Brian Nolan, for their love and their care. Throughout my life they have always encouraged me to follow my interests and they have supported me across numerous endeavours, in academia and beyond. This book is dedicated to them.

Glossary

bao	reciprocity
Caijing	highly regarded financial and economics journal (published in Chinese and English)
caipiao	chop loans
ganqing	sentiment
guanxi	connections
guanxi xue	the practice of exchanging gifts and favours to strengthen personal ties
Kuomintang	Nationalist Party of China
li	propriety in personal conduct, important in Confucian ethics
Manchukuo	puppet state established by the Japanese in Northeast China and Inner Mongolia (1932–1945)
mianzi	face
qianzhuang	money shops
renqing	human feelings
taizidang	'princelings', relatives of senior officials
xianjin	advanced (in relation to technologies and economic systems)
xixueweiyong	Western learning as function
yinhang	modern Chinese bank
Yinghangjia zazhi	Chinese Banker Magazine
yuguojijiegui	'linking up with the international track'
zhongxueweiti	Chinese learning as essence

Abbreviations

ABC	Agricultural Bank of China
ACCC	American Chamber of Commerce in China
AFC	Asian Financial Crisis
AMC	asset management company
BCBS	Basel Committee on Banking Supervision
BOC	Bank of China
CAMELS	capital adequacy, asset quality, management, earnings, liquidity ratios and sensitivity to market risk
CBRC	China Banking Regulatory Commission
CCB	China Construction Bank
CCP	Chinese Communist Party
CDIC	Central Discipline Inspection Committee
CIA	Council of International Advisors
EUCCC	European Union Chamber of Commerce in China
FCPA	Foreign Corrupt Practices Act
FDI	foreign direct investment
G-20	informal group of 19 countries and the European Union
GDP	gross domestic product
GITIC	Guangdong International Trust and Investment Corporation
HRM	human resource management
HSBC	Hong Kong and Shanghai Banking Corporation
IBC	Imperial Bank of China
ICBC	Industrial and Commercial Bank of China
ICCM	international and cross-cultural management
IFC	International Finance Corporation
IIF	Institute of International Finance
IMF	International Monetary Fund
IPO	initial public offering
ITIC	international trust and investment corporation
JSCB	joint stock commercial bank
KMT	Kuomintang (nationalist party of China)
MGI	McKinsey Global Institute
MNC	multinational corporation

NPL	non-performing loans
PBC	People's Bank of China
PRC	People's Republic of China
PWC	PricewaterhouseCoopers
RBS	Royal Bank of Scotland
RMB	*Renminbi* (currency of the PRC)
SASAC	State-owned Assets Supervision and Administration Commission
SEC	Security and Exchange Commission
SME	small and medium-size enterprises
SOB	state-owned bank
SOCB	state-owned Commercial Bank
SOE	state-owned enterprises
WTO	World Trade Organization

1 Introduction

Western bankers in China

In the early 1990s, China's banks were crippled by debt and on the edge of bankruptcy, now they are among the largest and most profitable organizations in the world (Palma, 2017). What processes lie behind this dramatic change?

We hear different answers from different disciplinary voices. Economists point to macro-level interventions such as the recapitalization of the state-owned banks in the late 1990s, the introduction of new governance structures influenced by Western economic thinking, and the opening up of the sector to foreign strategic investment (Cousin, 2011; Gewirtz, 2017). Others argue that China's rise up the profitability rankings occurred, in large part, because of the collapse of Western banks during the financial crisis which began in 2008–2009 (Löchel & Li, 2011). In this book, we offer another level of analysis through examining the encounters between Chinese and Western managers in the banking sector and their organizational practices. We argue that while the very act of allowing foreign bank entry may have been based on a policy decision aimed at creating greater efficiencies in the banking system, this is not what is observed at the organizational level. Indeed, the book will show that the very term 'efficiencies' is a contested concept, constructed in different ways by different economic actors in the study. We will show how relationships between Chinese and Western managers are influenced by the shifting economic landscapes, power relations, political decisions, cultural milieus and social networks in which they are embedded. Convergence between the two groups towards a common socio-economic order, we will argue, is unlikely. We hypothesize that the Chinese administration will seek to develop their own 'national champions' in the banking sector and will keep the influence of Western banks firmly in check. This will occur both through continuing government support for the large former state-owned banks and strategies aimed at protecting small domestic city banks from foreign domination. While Chinese banks may, in time, seek to penetrate Western financial markets, for the foreseeable future any outward movement is likely to remain focused on developing nations in Africa and the Asia Pacific region nations (Buckley et al., 2018; Pilling, 2017).

Setting the scene

Prior to the start of the reform period in the early 1980s, the Chinese banking sector was organized around a 'monobank' system where the People's Bank of China (PBC) assumed numerous functions including those of a commercial bank, a banking supervisor and a government treasury (Cousin, 2011). The then 'command economy' set up after 1949, was based on the Soviet model under the leadership of Mao Zedong (1893–1976). Famously, his successor, Deng Xiaoping (1904–1997) was quoted as saying that Chinese banks needed to be turned into 'real banks', because they were simply 'money printing enterprises, cash vaults' (Jing, 2005, cited in Cousin, 2007, p. 4). Initial changes in the sector in the 1980s and 1990s included separating the commercial function of PBC into four state-owned commercial banks (SOCBs), establishing policy banks and asset management companies, and developing a legal framework suitable for financial services (Cousin, 2011).

After several further periods of reform, and as part of the terms of its accession to the World Trade Organization (WTO) in 2001, China made a commitment to open its banking sector more fully to foreign competition in late 2006. This promise continues to be ongoing – up to the present date. The lead-up to accession was regarded by some Chinese officials as a chance to radically modernize the domestic banking sector (Brahm, 2002). Foreign banks were viewed as part of the 'solution' because it was assumed they could, through joint ventures, assist local banks with the development of new technologies, financial products and management techniques. There was also a general view that foreign banks would help enhance the corporate governance of local banks, both directly (through joint ventures and shareholdings in Chinese banks) and indirectly (through creating competitive pressures in the domestic market) (Cousin, 2007, 2011). The present leadership in China, at least in its public statements, appears to be in favour of deepening the economic reforms, the banking sector notwithstanding.

In the early and mid-2000s, Chinese banking regulators sent out encouraging messages to foreign banks about the potential for a 'win win' scenario. While the foreign bank would get access to some of the profits to be made from the vast customer networks of Chinese banks, they would also help the local banks: 'improve their corporate governance, internal controls, information disclosure and financial management' (CBRC, 2005, p. 15). There are now clear indicators of change in many of these areas. The regulatory system is moving towards risk-based supervision, and the separation of duties and responsibilities between PBC and the China Banking Regulatory Commission (CBRC) in 2003 has encouraged higher levels of specialization and expertise (Cousin, 2011). At the level of the firm, Chinese banks are more and more developing the retail financial products suitable for capitalist systems (such as mortgages, personal loans and credit cards) and the commercial and investment banking sectors are becoming more sophisticated (PricewaterhouseCoopers, 2016). Support from the International Monetary Fund (IMF) through technical assistance projects has helped improve accounting systems and has encouraged, at a surface level, greater convergence on international practices in this particular area (Hamid & Tenev, 2008). In one sense, therefore, it is clear that Chinese banks have indeed been adopting the banking techniques found in Western capitalist economies and have specifically sought out Western bankers to act as change agents in modernizing the sector. Numerous studies have investigated the effects of these changes in terms of their effect on the financial landscape in China at the macro level (Cousin, 2011; Löchel & Li, 2011). However, much less attention has been focused on how these state-level policy decisions have been interpreted by the economic actors who have been actively involved in the transition. In this book, we investigate institutional and organizational change in the banking sector by studying, at the organizational level, the multiple ways in which key economic actors have experienced the reforms. In doing so, we aim to show that managers and executives do not passively follow through on the top-down edicts of policy-makers. On the contrary, they transform and adapt them, sometimes disregard them and occasionally even sabotage them in ways which make an analysis of power relations a core explanatory theme.

A comparative business systems approach

In order to understand the perspectives of Chinese and Western actors on the dramatic changes which have occurred in the banking sector, we will use a *comparative business systems approach* as an organizing framework (Redding, 2005). At its most fundamental level, this is concerned with investigating why business organization and economic action varies in different societies (Redding & Witt, 2007; Witt & Redding, 2013). Drawing on insights developed in earlier work (Child, 2000; Whitley, 1992), Redding (2005) develops *a model which integrates three core levels of analysis: culture and meaning, institutional order, and firm co-ordination.* He also examines the interaction between the three different levels and highlights the importance of developing an historical approach to understanding business systems, to examining the role of interest groups in motivating certain forms of economic action, and to mapping the complexities of the material and ideational 'logics' that are adopted by key actors.

In this book we will draw on Redding's model which we hope to modify and extend to explain what happens at the organizational level when two different business systems in banking, one developed in the West and one emerging in China, come into contact. In doing so, we will develop our own theoretical contribution regarding the role of *power relations* and *sources of conflict* in an emerging system.

The kinds of questions we wish to answer include the following: How does state-level policy influence the meaning attached to new banking regulations by different actors, interest groups and organizations (Chapter 5)? Have joint ventures and foreign investments improved the corporate governance of Chinese banks and what kind of corporate governance model is emerging in the sector (Chapter 6)? What role do Chinese power–money social networks play in the networking strategies of Western bankers at the organizational level (Chapter 7)? How did the 2008 financial crisis influence levels of confidence and trust between Western and Chinese bankers (Chapter 8)?

To answer these questions, it is important to develop an organizational-level analysis which is both historically embedded and focused on how power relations and ideational factors construct the strategies and practices adopted by managers. This requires an epistemological position that 'pursues understanding via description' rather than 'proof via positivism' (Redding, 2005, p. 124). In this book, we aim to build a thick description based on an interpretivist perspective using data gleaned through in-depth interviews and document analysis. Many have noted that the field of international business and management will not usefully benefit from yet more values-based large-scale surveys of cross-cultural interaction which are too often focused on narrow, trivial questions which 'factor out' contextual information as inconvenient statistical 'noise' (Child, 2009; Jack & Westwood, 2009). To quote McSweeney (2002, p. 113), we now need studies 'that can cope with change, power, variety, multiple influences, including the non-national – and the complexity and situational variability of the individual subject'. As we will discuss in Chapter 2, it is essential now to considers cases as historically situated; to foreground the socially constructed nature of terms such as 'competition' and 'efficiency' overturning rationalist economic assumptions that such concepts have universal applicability; to acknowledge relations of power both between and within states, highlighting the importance of elite interest groups; and, importantly, to provide a sophisticated and dynamic view of 'culture' which goes beyond the static conceptualizations found in most contemporary management research (McSweeney, 2002; Redding, 2005; Redding & Witt, 2007).

A study of the Chinese banking sector

Between 2008 and 2011, interviews were conducted with 60 executives, public officials and senior managers from 12 different banks in mainland China, over the period of the financial crisis. These included Western and Chinese employees who were working in state-owned banks, joint-venture banks or Western-owned banks. In addition, we examined official documents from a number of key interest groups in the banking sector including the CBRC, the European and American Chambers of Commerce in China, as well as policy documents issued by the banks themselves and official state press releases. The latter documents may be taken as *representations* of official positions and can be usefully compared and contrasted with the actual day-to-day experiences described by participants. We have maintained an ongoing brief with respect to changes in the sector up to the present time of writing.

An in-depth discussion of the sample and methods can be found in the Methodological Appendix. Western-owned banks are defined as those headquartered in North America, Europe and Australia. According to PricewaterhouseCoopers (PWC) (2008), these regions had the largest foreign presence in China's banking sector during the time of the research (and indeed continue to do so today) (PWC, 2014). Large global banks from these regions, such as HSBC and Bank of America, have, historically speaking, had the most involvement in the Chinese banking industry, with connections dating back to the late-Qing dynasty during the 1860s. Consequently, they perceived themselves as well placed to negotiate for close involvement in the post-1978 banking reforms and were given preferential treatment by Chinese officials. A timeline of the key historical events in the development of Chinese banks is shown in Table 1.1.

Global, transnational or Western banks?

There are important debates about the use of the term 'headquarter nation' as an identifier of the 'national' or 'regional' character of a bank. Many might

Table 1.1 Key historical events in the development of Chinese banks

Date	*Event*
960–1279	Oldest banks, Song Dynasty
1865	China's first central bank was established as the Bank of the Board of Revenue
1865	HSBC first opens doors in Shanghai
1897	Imperial Bank of China
1911	Nationalist revolution
1912	Bank of China
1937–1948	War
1949	The Liberation
1949	People's Bank of China
1984	ISBC founded
1986	Great Wall credit card
1978	Deng's reforms
1979	BOC separates from PBOC
1995	China Development Bank
1997	Asia Financial Crisis
2000	WTO entry
2006–2007	Foreign banks expansion
2008	Great Financial Crisis
2009	Credit expansion package
2017	One Belt, One Road
2017	Xi's Davos Speech
2017	New rules on foreign banks

prefer to describe these large global banks as 'transnational' institutions of enormous global power who are not confined by conventional geographical borders or nation-state control (Mander, 2014; Robinson, 2012). It is certainly true that they can effectively lobby for free access to markets and light touch regulation in many regions of the globe (Harris, 2012; Young, 2013). As such, the question is raised as to whether the very term 'international' is now a term with outdated assumptions? Has the concept of 'global' become *de rigueur*? In China, however, where political and cultural narratives emphasize the importance of a strong state and China's national distinctiveness, 'global' banks simply do not enjoy the same freedoms they may experience elsewhere (Callahan, 2014; Freeman & Yuan, 2012). Moreover, at the organizational and individual level, a friction between the two groups is clearly observable, not just in policy discourse but in the perspectives and experiences of managers and executives themselves. As such, making the conceptual distinction between Chinese and Western banks is a valid one for this study.[1]

The 2008 banking crisis

When planning this study, we had not anticipated that it would happen during one of the biggest crises in the history of global banking since the 1930s. We had originally been interested in investigating how institutional reforms in China were being experienced in the tertiary professional services sector. This was because much previous research had focused on China's transition from a rural to an urban economy and on the growth of manufacturing. The opening up of the banking sector in late 2006 provided a unique opportunity to investigate how, at the organizational level, China might develop a 'knowledge economy' as part of its goal to move up the global value-chain (Altenburg, Schmitz & Stamm, 2008). We were especially interested in the themes of business networks and international legitimacy-seeking in Chinese banks as they began to engage with the global financial sector through initial public offerings (IPOs), joint ventures and technical assistance projects (Cousin, 2011; Guthrie, 2001; Hamid & Tenev, 2008). The financial crisis which began in 2007, shortly before we started the interviews, introduced a new set of dynamics to the project. Tremendous strain was placed on the credibility of the Western banks themselves, and there was a deep questioning among some Chinese officials of the rationale for allowing them entry to the Chinese market in the first place.

The 2008 financial crisis put the authority of key Western economic assumptions, which had been so keenly observed and admired by some earlier Chinese officials (Brahm, 2002), to the most severe test (Xin, 2008). According to the Nobel laureate Joseph Stiglitz (2010), one of the key reasons for the crisis was the wholesale backing by US policy-makers of the principles of free market 'fundamentalism', specifically the de-regulation and liberalization of the financial sector. While certainly not describing themselves as 'fundamentalist', prior to the crisis certain voices in the Chinese administration had echoed similar support for liberalizing China's financial sector and indeed this had been a key rationale for allowing foreign banks entry to the Chinese market in the first place (Brahm, 2002; Cousin, 2011). There is no doubt, however, that the financial crisis gave voice to those in the Chinese government who had always been resistant to the banking reforms, and particularly the extent to which 'outsiders' should be allowed access to China's domestic banking sector. Much of this dialogue came from those on the 'left' of China's political spectrum who were concerned about the implications this may have for China's financial security and economic sovereignty (Freeman & Yuan, 2011; Naughton, 2006). These debates were circulating widely at the time of the study, in both Western and Chinese media. It was clear that they were important to the participants in this study and influenced their day-to-day encounters and organizational practices.[2]

An outline of the book

We begin Chapter 2 by considering the relationship between cultural values and capitalist development, highlighting the influence of this research on international and cross-cultural management studies in China. We also introduce the key institutional perspectives that have been used to explain China's economic and organizational reforms and outline contemporary critiques of 'new' institutionalism. Chapter 3 introduces the *comparative business system approach* which we use to introduce specific contextual information and important explanatory concepts, both of which inform the empirical data presented in later chapters. We also discuss the implications of the model, with its emphasis on culture, institutions and firm co-ordination, on divergence in management practice and organization in Chinese firms. Chapter 4 outlines key historical moments in the reform of the banking process, noting how past encounters with the West have often been problematic, creating an ambivalent attitude among Chinese managers and officials to what may be gained through co-operative initiatives. Chapter 5 examines the development of banking regulatory institutions and identifies ideological conflicts between Chinese and Western perspectives on the overall objective and purpose of regulations. Chapter 6 identifies the emergence of a Chinese model of corporate governance and describes shifts from initial concerns with international legitimacy-seeking towards the perceived ineffectiveness of Western non-executive directors. It examines the impact of enduring cultural preferences, such as a reliance on informal social networks (*guanxi*) on the trajectory of governance reforms. Chapter 7 investigates the networking strategies of Western managers and describes the perceived importance of hiring influential 'princelings' and other well-connected individuals in order to develop their interests in the banking sector. Chapter 8 examines institutional and organizational trust, making visible the consequences of the 2008 banking crisis for the reputations of Western institutions, executives and managers working in the Chinese banking sector. It maps the strategies and practices used by Chinese officials to curb Western influence in what can still be categorized as a low-trust environment.

Chapter 9 concludes by emphasizing that the specific practices and strategies identified in the study demonstrate that managers cannot simply be described as rational profit maximizers. They actively interpret and respond to their circumstances in a variety of ways which suggest there is likely to be continuing divergence and variety in socio-economic activity. The experiences of participants are best understood by reference to state-influenced institutional histories, power relations and cultural dynamics. These factors shape the organizational forms which are now emerging as China seeks to reassert its position in the global arena in the new era of what the current leader, Xi Jinping, has dubbed the 'China Dream'.

Chapter 2: Understanding institutional and organizational change in Chinese contexts

In this chapter we examine the relationship between cultural values, capitalist development and patterns of global divergence in economic action. We also evaluate some of the key institutional perspectives, mostly US-driven, which have been used to explain China's economic reforms to date. These emerged in the period after the reforms were introduced in the People's Republic of China (PRC) and cover a wide range of literature. Institutional approaches became very popular in China and permeate a good deal of its economic writings. Finally, we outline contemporary critiques of 'new' institutionalism which argue for the necessity of developing the framework by introducing more nuanced understandings of power relations at the organizational level.

Chapter 3: The variety of business systems in China's banking sector

We then introduce Redding's (2005) model of comparative business systems analysis. We develop and extend these ideas through a more detailed focus on power relations. As noted earlier, the model has three levels: culture, institutions and rules of co-ordination. Each level, in turn, consists of three parts (Witt & Redding, 2013). Culture is defined as the 'social construction of reality' (Berger & Luckmann, 1966) and consists of three elements, namely rationale, identity and authority. Institutions, in this particular model, refer to the rules which govern three different kinds of capital: financial, human and social. Rules of co-ordination signify the nature of ownership patterns, co-operation across firms (relatively rare in China) and the kinds of management practices used within firms. We illustrate each core concept with examples relevant to the current study. Overarching each level of the model are the complex 'rationales' used by the state itself which have emerged in a specific historical context.

In China, the state still retains a strong grip on the economy in reality, both through the ownership structures of strategic industries (including banking and finance) and through the development of regulatory frameworks which ostensibly support social and economic stabilities as well as the promotion of business 'efficiencies'. These factors, which have emerged in a region which takes great pride in its distinctive cultural heritage, undermine any simple notion of convergence in either surface-level regulatory design or organizational-level management practice. The Chinese ruling elite is reluctant to give up control and this represents a fundamental problem with respect to the extension of market-driven forces.

Chapter 4: Western economic ideas and the historical development of Chinese banks

Chapter 4 introduces the historical context of banking reforms in China, outlining specifically the role of Western banks. Following a brief review of the expansion and dominance of foreign banks between 1840 and 1949, we move on to discuss the fate of the banking sector during the 30-year period of communist 'self-sufficiency' (1949–1978) and the subsequent legacy of the vast non-performing loans (NPLs) created by the state-owned enterprises (SOEs). We then examine the policy rationale for allowing foreign banks to re-enter the system in the 1980s and discuss the nature of the organizational field in which Western banks now operate in China. A key theme in this chapter will be to foreground the historical and cultural forces which continue to influence the banking system today and to draw attention to the ambiguous role played by Western bankers: sources of potentially useful technical knowledge and potential threat to Chinese values and economic security. This duality may be partly understood through examining the particular narrative of history which is promoted by the Chinese Communist Party (CCP) as it seeks to maintain its legitimacy throughout the reform period. We conclude by describing the level of Western involvement in the sector during the period of the study (focusing specifically on investments in 2010) and by identifying some of the initial reactions of Chinese officials to the emerging banking crisis, many of which referred to the West's past behaviour in China. A timeline of key events in the development of China's banking sector is provided in Table 1.1.

Chapter 5: Regulating the banking sector: conflict and control in enforcement regimes

In this chapter, we examine three main issues. First, we investigate the rationale used by the CBRC for adopting elements of international banking regulation. Second, we map the perceptions of Western managers on the effectiveness of these regulations at the organizational level. Finally, we outline the struggle for control over the social values and economic ideas which are shaping the emerging regulatory field. While the architecture of current regulation indicates a degree of international convergence in China's banking regulations, the 'cherry-picking' approach of the regulator is perceived by Western managers as displaying a protectionist sentiment. They protest by reiterating, through formal and informal channels, the assumed universal benefits of market competition and the belief that it will always create greater organizational efficiencies. They note, too, a general lack of co-ordination and organization between Chinese authorities which compounds their difficulties. The relationship between the Chinese regulator, international organizations (such as the WTO and the Basel Committee) and Western executives offers a clear example of conflict and struggle between key economic actors, not just at the level of material resources but at the level of ideas and cultural values, where specific interpretive frames are used to justify individual, organizational and regulatory action. Since 2008, prominent Chinese officials have become increasingly vocal about the limits of Western 'laissez-faire' approaches to regulation, noting that it might not be appropriate for Chinese cultures where 'social stability' is asserted to be a more highly valued goal than in the West.

Chapter 6: Western investors and corporate governance reforms in Chinese banks

In Chapter 6, we show that while there has been relatively rapid change in the governance environment, informal cultural practices at the organizational level are changing at a much slower pace. Components of Western models of corporate governance such as the Board of Directors and diversified ownership structures have certainly been widely adopted by Chinese banks. However, the overriding perception of participants was that the motivation for pursuing these changes had been legitimacy-seeking by Chinese banks in the global financial environment prior to the banking crisis which began in 2007. In practice, however, the enduring importance of informal social networks, such as *guanxi*, in gaining access to credit means that the overall influence of Western banks on corporate governance reforms in China is perceived by participants as usually ineffective.

A Chinese-style 'control-based' model of corporate governance, where the state intervenes in the banking sector to ensure financial stability and the achievement of social objectives such as employment and enterprise support, is clearly evident. In general terms, the system is said to remain burdened by corruption and rent-seeking, which cannot be justified simply on the basis of enduring cultural preferences. Instead, it points to the enduring influence and power of key elements of China's political elite, many of whom are officially under investigation by the current Party leadership.

Chapter 7: Networking strategies of Western bankers: power, opportunism and **guanxi** *connections*

As noted in earlier chapters, the regulatory environment in China is pitted against Western banks, partly through some elements of formal regulation but more significantly through informal processes aimed at undermining and obstructing their efforts to establish themselves in the sector. This chapter examines perceptions of so-called 'relationship hires' among Western banks operating in China and outlines the influence of 'princelings' in the banking sector more generally. We demonstrate how Western executives seek to access local '*guanxi*' networks in order to assist them in gaining regulatory approval and expanding their customer networks. Several different strategies emerge, each justified in different ways. Some managers refer to the importance of *guanxi* as a 'unique' Chinese cultural characteristic, which must be cultivated as part of establishing any business. Others take a more instrumental approach, noting the specific nature of 'political' *guanxi* in China and its roots in a particular institutional and historical context. *Guanxi* is viewed as an outcome of an institutional system where the rule of law is weak and elite influence is entrenched. In order to negotiate this environment, *guanxi* connections are needed and the recruitment of well-connected local Chinese into the system is deemed essential. The implications of this for both reform in the Chinese banking sector and for the development of foreign competition are discussed.

Chapter 8: The 2008 financial crisis and trust between Chinese and Western bankers

This chapter will examine the socially constructed nature of trust between Chinese and Western managers. China is sometimes characterized as a 'low-trust' environment in that, for cultural and historical reasons, trust in both non-Chinese individuals and formal institutions tends to be low (Fukuyama, 1995). In this chapter, we develop a more nuanced picture. In one sense, the abilities of Western bankers to design sophisticated financial products contributed, initially, to establishing their credibility in the sector (certainly prior to the banking crisis). In other words, their financial knowledge constituted a key element of their 'symbolic capital' in the banking field in China and inspired trust in their technical capabilities (Bourdieu, 1986). That said, at the organizational level, individual Western managers involved in technical assistance projects were viewed, by the Chinese participants in this study at least, as culturally insensitive, lacking an appreciation of China as a particularist and collectivist society. Moreover, there was a general perception that Western banks, as institutions, constituted a potential threat to China's economic security. We go on to examine a range of practices and strategies adopted by Chinese officials and managers which demonstrate a distinct lack of trust in Western banks in many quarters we investigated. These include attempts at data raiding, obstructing and delaying the issuing of licences, and sabotaging co-operation agreements. We will also show how the reputational damage suffered by Western banks during the banking crisis reconfirmed existing beliefs among Chinese managers that Western institutions lack long-term commitment to China. Sometimes, allegations of 'cheating', 'tricking' and 'lack of respect' are themes used by Chinese executives and managers to describe the actions of some of their Western counterparts.

Chapter 9: Conclusions and implications

China has a long history of 'learning from the West' in relation to acquiring technical and scientific knowledge (Spence, 1990; Wang, 2007; Warner, 2017). However, one of the key features of China's ambitions over the past 100 years has been to resist both perceived and actual manipulation by Western powers and to reassert itself into a respected position in the global arena (Bickers, 2017; Callahan, 2014; Zhao, 1997). Bickers (2017) provides a robust historical account of how China was able to throw off the legacy of humiliation, to go on to become the world's second largest economic entity.

In the concluding chapter, we emphasize that, in the specific case of managers in the Chinese banking sector, there remains a degree of ambiguity towards Western banks. It is certainly possible to identify policy statements aimed at developing the sector through technical assistance projects, joint ventures and allowing some foreign competition in the sector. However, we show that the day-to-day practices of Chinese managers and officials may aim to keep foreign influence in check and to obstruct the ability of Western banks to progress.

Managers themselves do not passively respond to top-down policies, from either their own headquarters or from local or national government. There is no doubt that the banking sector is of great strategic importance for China's development; however, a full understanding of the sector, and its future prospects, can only be reached by investigating the perspectives of managers at the organizational level. Managers make decisions not simply because they are 'rational profit maximizers' but because they are embedded in socially constructed organizations which in turn are enmeshed in long-standing cultural influence and historically situated institutions.

Notes

1 We acknowledge the important influence of other foreign banks on China's banking sector, especially those from elsewhere in East Asia including Japan, Korea, Taiwan and Hong Kong. However, for this study, which is focused specifically on China's encounter with Western-dominated institutions, they are not discussed in detail. For stylistic reasons, we may occasionally use the term 'foreign' bank, but this should be taken, in the main, as referring to Western banks.

2 The concept 'practice' is used in different ways in different theoretical models. It can, somewhat confusingly, be referenced as cause, effect and explanation (Gad & Jensen, 2014; Morgan, Edwards & Gomes, 2014). In this study, 'practice' refers to what actors actually do and also to what they say they do. In other words, 'practice' is a research object.

2 Understanding institutional and organizational change in Chinese contexts

The transition from communist central planning to state-controlled capitalism in China has often been described as a gradual, experimental process; in the words of Deng Xiaoping (1904–1997), China is 'groping for stones to cross the river' (Lin, Cai & Li, 2003, p. 177). This pattern contrasts markedly with the nature of communist transition in Russia and Eastern Europe which was based on a radical, 'shock therapy' approach (Edwards et al., 2005). Here, the aim was to drive dramatic and sudden change across a range of political, social and economic institutions (Buck et al., 2001; P. H. Nolan, 1995; Stiglitz, 2014). These two different approaches to reform, 'gradualism' vs 'shock therapy', have raised many arguments and debates about the relative influence of indigenous culture, local elites and politics on institutional and organizational change. More specifically, there is a long-standing debate over the extent to which the assumptions of neo-classical institutional economics can have universal applicability. In brief, is it really possible that free market competition releases human potential and inevitably creates 'improvements' in both economic performance and social well-being in all political and cultural contexts? (Popov, 2000; Sachs & Woo, 1994; Stiglitz, 2014). To explore this question, we will first consider the relationship between cultural values, capitalist development and patterns of global divergence in economic action. In doing so, we will outline the importance of this debate to many of the assumptions we encounter in studies of international and cross-cultural management (ICCM). We will then introduce the key institutional perspectives that have been used to explain China's economic and organizational reforms. Finally, we will outline contemporary critiques of 'new' institutionalism which argue for the urgent need to develop more nuanced understandings of power relations at the organizational level. This development has real potential for developing our understanding of how change, and stability, occurs at the organizational level in China's banking sector, key themes of later empirical chapters.

Cultural values and capitalist development

The German sociologist Max Weber (1864–1871) wrote extensively on the role of cultural values in comparative capitalist development. His work is often taken as the source for many of the core debates in ICCM (Jack & Westwood, 2009; Javidan et al., 2006). For example, in *The Protestant Ethic and the Spirit of Capitalism*, Weber (1905/2002) argues that Calvinistic thinking, which was premised on developing a personal relationship with an 'absent' God, encouraged a form of individualist subjectivity in European Protestant countries, which, over time, created a society and economy that is ordered and controlled by abstract laws. In the West, Weber argues, this pattern supported the development of a type of capitalism based on rational action and rule-based bureaucracy. Similarly, in *The Religion of China: Confucianism and Taoism* (1915/1968), he argues that Chinese civilization is characterized as one largely free of monotheistic religious beliefs and is based, instead, on a set of principles which prioritize natural harmonies and hierarchies in relationships.

A number of commentators have been influenced by Weber's observations and have argued that East Asian capitalisms, and their associated institutions and organizations, are less concerned with formal and abstract rules, at least when compared with their Western counterparts (Hamilton, 2006; Redding & Witt, 2007; Warner, 2014a). Hamilton (2006) claims that Weber's key insight into understanding the emergence of capitalism was to show how 'civilizational worldviews', especially philosophical and religious beliefs, influence other spheres of life through encouraging the development of specific forms of cultural values and authority relationships.

Weber's work introduced many of the core assumptions about the relationship between culture, society and economy which continue to structure the field of ICCM today. Not least among these is that management researchers frequently define 'culture' itself as a 'values' concept (Weber, 1904/2011). For example, in recent decades, Geert Hofstede (1984, 2001, 2011) has argued that it is possible to classify countries along an 'individualism' vs 'collectivism' dimension. According to Hofstede, individualism is found in societies (such as the USA) in which the ties between individuals are loose and the core emotional obligations are to look after oneself and immediate family. Collectivism, in contrast, is found in societies in which people are bound to specific 'in-groups' across the life course (as, for example, in China). These basic patterns are reflected in preferences for different kinds of organization and management practices. Hofstede's model is not without its critics (Jack & Westwood 2009; McSweeney, 2002) and we will evaluate the limitations of the model, and its definition of 'culture', in more detail in Chapter 3. That said, it has to be acknowledged that Hofstede's 'dimensional' approach to cultural values remains one of the most influential models in ICCM, proving particularly popular with researchers specializing in management research in Asian societies (Warner 2014b).

Convergence and divergence in material and ideational factors

Much of the early research in ICCM was concerned with studying the internationalization processes of US firms and the cultural and institutional differences they encountered during that process (Boyacigiller & Adler, 1991; Jack & Westwood, 2009) and is thus biased in this direction. The literature is dominated by concerns with how US businesses could operate successfully in diverse cultural conditions, but there was an overall assumption that the process of industrialization itself was inevitable (Adler & Boyacigiller, 1996). The 'industrialization thesis' so-called (Harbison & Myers, 1959; Kerr, Dunlop & Harbison, 1960) assumed that all societies will eventually 'converge', or industrialize, because the overall advantages of such systems are so great. At one level, Kerr *et al.*'s (1960) thesis placed particular emphasis on the influence of *material factors* in creating changes in cultural values. As societies modernize their economic and technological activities, the division of labour becomes more complex and this encourages the development of efficiency-based organizational rules and codified knowledge (Child, 2009). Weber had identified this process in his earlier work, noting that modernization (which also includes industrialization) may lead to social routines which require *formal rationality* – that is, a kind of decision-making based on technical criteria or calculations which, ostensibly, eliminate value judgements (Weber, 1947/2009). In other words, as Jack and Westwood (2009) note, the industrialization hypothesis assumed that *convergence* would occur not just in economies, institutions and organizations, but also in value orientations. This has been underpinned by a teleological position that assumed the diminishing of cultural 'difference' and the development of 'affective neutrality' where rational, instrumental modes of subjectivity, organization and management eventually become universalized. In brief, the thesis was that industrialization brings with it 'an increase in universalism, achievement, suppression of immediate emotional release (affective neutrality) and specificity' (Jack & Westwood, 2009, p. 137).

While there was an assumption in the industrialization thesis that material factors would inevitably lead to value change, it is now apparent that *ideational factors* continue to interact with the industrialization processes in diverse ways around the globe (see Rowley, 2017). In the 1980s, Gary Hamilton and his colleagues argued that Western theories of modernization, with their emphasis on the rise of the democratic nation-state, the rule of law and the institutionalization of *property rights*, seemed strikingly inadequate for explaining the growth and stability of strong capitalist economies in East Asia (Hamilton, 1990). Returning to Weber (1947/2009), Child (2009) notes that ideational factors may be related to political ideologies, such as communism, as well as to philosophical and religious values such as the continuation of different forms of *substantive rationality* which are concerned with the differing values that people attach to social and economic organization. In China, management practices may be driven by substantive rationalities based on Confucian ethics and ideologies such as propriety (*li*) and 'moral' leadership (Child, 2009; Warner, 2016). Management decision-making in global management may, therefore, vary according to the ethical norms of any given society, and cannot be reduced entirely to the *material* nature of organizational objectives. In other words, 'rationality' and rational action is context-specific and may not, in a business context, always be strictly concerned with profit maximization and the creation of an 'efficient' organization. The importance of context cannot be overestimated.

In relation to the study of management in China, a recent study identifies a specific form of 'Confucian' human resource management (HRM) which may be derived from the cultural values of Confucianism, such as the emphasis on societal order and hierarchy which encourages harmonious relationships and vertical authority linkages in the workplace (Warner, 2014c). Such preferences can create significant differences from management practices commonly found in Western organizations. For example, in relation to HRM procedures, processes such as recruitment, appraisal and promotion may be based on strong personal connections (*guanxi*) and age seniority rather than personal performance, work experience or educational attainment (Gu & Nolan, 2017; Warner, 2014c). Nevertheless, despite the clear possibility that Chinese organizations and management practices diverge from those found in the West, it still remains possible to identify elements of 'convergence' and 'formal rationality' in certain areas of China's economy, positing a new hybrid economic and managerial system.

Contemporary examples of formal rationality in China that are relevant to this study include state-level policy decisions such as joining the WTO, implementing the Basel III global capital standards,[1] and the adoption of organizational forms such as the joint-stock company. A US-based contributor to the debate, Doug Guthrie (1998; 2001), is particularly keen to emphasize that the evolution of 'rational-legal' structures in China may be reducing the influence of personalized patron–client relationships in the workplace (what is sometimes referred to as *guanxi* recruitment, a theme of Chapter 7). Whether or not Guthrie has been somewhat precipitate in his claims will be discussed in later chapters. However, it is certainly fair to say that there have been a number of institutional changes in China which do seem to resemble a move towards the rational-bureaucratic systems and legal frameworks found in Western market economies. In order to understand this shift in more detail it is necessary to consider what forms of institutional analysis have been used, to date, to explain reforms in China's economy and management practice and to consider how well they account for processes of change and stability.

Institutional analyses of Chinese economy and management

In the contemporary field of institutional analysis, it is possible to differentiate between theorists who focus on how change is driven by sudden, external events or 'exogenous shocks' (e.g. severe economic recessions, natural disasters and violent conflicts) and those who examine the ways in which institutions slowly modify over time through processes of path dependency (Mahoney & Thelen, 2010). Each different approach prioritizes different behavioural assumptions (such as the degree to which rational action is shaped by context), and foregrounds different sources of institutional change (e.g. transaction-cost economizing, elite interests, state regulations, collective action, social networks, individual and group norms, and so on). As Morgan, Edwards and Gomes (2014) note, it is now possible to identify at last four types of institutionalism: rational choice institutionalism, historical institutionalism, sociological or organizational institutionalism and, more recently, discursive institutionalism (Hall & Taylor, 1996; Schmidt, 2008, 2010). Most of these perspectives would agree that an 'institution' encompasses both the informal beliefs and behaviours of a given society and the formal organizations and state rules that govern those beliefs and behaviours. Where they would disagree, however, is about which particular processes are the most fundamental driving forces behind institutional change. Some give explanatory power to the influence of political elites and international organizations (such as the IMF and WTO); others foreground the importance of embedded cultural preferences. Moreover, critics of institutional theory argue that the concept of 'power' has not been fully utilized, especially in the kind of organizational institutionalism which has emerged in North American business schools (Clegg, 2010; Willmott, 2015).

In the sections below, we will illustrate how different kinds of institutionalism have been used to study economic reforms and management practices in China, drawing out some of the key concepts used to describe both change and stability. We will conclude with a review of why business and management research may benefit from a much closer engagement with broader social science debates about power relations, a standpoint that we adopt in this study.

Rational choice institutionalism

The assumptions of rational choice or 'neo-classical' approaches to institutional change has broad affinities with the industrialization thesis introduced earlier (Kerr *et al.*, 1960). Specifically, rational choice institutionalism is premised on the belief that, in a global arena, institutions tend to converge, or become similar in form, because markets create incentives for actors to replace poor institutions with more efficient ones. Actors will learn how to improve their performance by modelling the behaviour of institutions that can survive in the face of market competition (North, 1981; Weingast, 2002). In other words, 'efficient' institutions in some way or another promote rational, self-interested behaviours which subsequently reduce transaction costs (Williamson, 1981). The work of the American economics scholar, Jeffrey Sachs, is an interesting example of the rational choice approach as applied to economic institutional change in China (Guthrie, 2001). Sachs's position is that institutional convergence towards the economic systems found in Western Europe, Japan and the US has been one of the key driving forces behind China's growth (Sachs & Woo, 2003). In his view, the fact that the Chinese government voluntarily sought membership of the WTO is a public recognition both of their belief in the utility of these models and of their intention to lead China into further harmonization with advanced economies.

Certainly, since the early 1990s, the majority of Chinese policy-makers have been in agreement that the modernization process must rest on the development of a 'market economy', borrowing from Western economic ideas (Brahm, 2002; Gewirtz, 2017). Given that Western industrialized nations have had the longest history of this form of economic activity, and are therefore viewed, by most Chinese officials, as the most 'advanced' (*xianjin*) in this activity, pursing an understanding of their economic systems and management methods has been an important policy goal (Wang, 2007). It is important to note, however, that these policy objectives relate principally to reforms in technical and economic realms, not in cultural or political ones, where the Chinese 'essence' must stay primary (Wang, 2007). Indeed, economic reform in China is exemplified in the policy slogan 'link up with the international track' (*yuguo jijie gui*) which, metaphorically, serves to compare China to a dynamic train rapidly moving forward and integrating with the international community. However, while it is possible to observe a number of state-level policy changes in China that seem to show convergence towards the rational-bureaucratic systems found in Western market economies, there are limits to what this approach can tell us. Critics of rational choice intuitionalism point to the relative lack of attention given to such matters as cultural variations in risk preferences and the goals of historically embedded dominant elites, as well as an enduring tendency to treat firms as homogenous 'black boxes' with little attention paid to the dynamics of internal organizational processes (Jack & Westwood, 2009; Redding, 2005). These variables have received greater attention from researchers influenced by sociological, organizational and historical institutionalism (as discussed below).

Sociological and organizational institutionalism

Sociological and organizational institutionalism seeks to understand the ways in which pre-existing social and institutional arrangements, which may be embedded in interpersonal ties, networks and cultural beliefs, have an enduring influence on China's economic transition, contributing to path dependency processes (Guthrie, 2001; Gold, Guthrie & Wank, 2002). In this framework, institutional change is not viewed principally as a product of rationalization, but, rather, is theorized as a gradually emerging outcome based on local 'social logics' which help actors 'make sense' of how they should act and behave within a given institutional context (Campbell, 2004; DiMaggio & Powell, 1983; Meyer & Rowan, 1977). Much work in this area is based on the assumption that what is 'rational' action is not universal but is highly dependent on *context*, an observation which, as discussed earlier, was initially made by Max Weber (1947/2009). The empirical focus of sociological and organizational institutionalism is usually on the micro-level practices which occur within and between organizations, and the beliefs and norms which guide the cognitions and decision-making processes of key actors (Scott, 2001). The argument runs that while organizations do indeed aim to survive in the face of competition, 'survival' need not simply mean economic success. It can also refer to a need to establish legitimacy in a specific 'field' of activity. 'Legitimacy' is, therefore, as much about survival in the *symbolic* realm as the material one, and consequently 'legitimacy seeking' is often used as a core explanatory concept for organizational and institutional change (Suddaby, 2010).

One interesting example of this approach is Guthrie's (2001) extensive study of the managers and directors of industrial organizations in Shanghai, conducted during the 1990s. He argued that the reason for 'convergence' on Western forms of management did not occur simply because managers believed these systems were more 'rational' and efficient. Rather, his findings seemed to indicate that Chinese managers 'mimicked' their foreign partners because they perceived them to be more 'saavy', and their management practices appeared, to them at least, to be more legitimate. In an environment where Chinese firms in some sectors were being 'set adrift' from central government, 'mimetic isomorphism' occurred because organizations in uncertain environments used their networks to copy the systems and procedures of those they perceived to be successful (DiMaggio & Powell, 1983). It was the aspiration to 'be like others' which drove the process of isomorphism (the general tendency of organizations to become similar in form).

Historical institutionalism

Historical institutionalists tend to define themselves as falling somewhere between the two positions discussed above. Steinmo (2008) notes that 'human beings are *both* norm-abiding rule followers *and* self-interested rational actors' (p. 163). Scholars in this field are generally concerned with examining significant political and social outcomes at a macro-level, drawing on case studies from the historical record. They tend to be less concerned with first-hand empirical investigations within organizations, which is largely the concern of sociological and organizational institutionalists (though see the work of Bell & Feng (2013) below). An interesting example, relevant to the concerns of this book, can be found in Guo's (2006) study of Asian transitions from communism. Guo argues that in order to understand *how* the economic reforms in China took the form they did, it is necessary to examine the tensions which existed between radical reformers and conservatives within the leadership group of the CCP during the 1980s. Through examining official documents from the period, Guo observed that while both groups often agreed that economic reform was necessary, tension occurred over the extent and degree of the transition. For example, when the CCP drafted a proposal for urban reform in 1984, Chen Yun (a conservative) suggested that a period of 30 years was appropriate. On the other hand, Hu Yaobang (a radical) argued that the reforms should occur over a much shorter period of around three to five years. Deng Xiaoping attempted to balance these two extremes over the course of his leadership (though he was often more accommodating to the conservative view). The continuous effort to reach a compromise between different factions contributed to the appearance of a 'two steps forward and one step back' pattern in China's reforms. When reform led to problems, such as inflation or dissident movements, the conservatives would blame the radicals, who would, in turn, be forced to defend their reforms and make concessions.

For Guo, this case study illustrates that the observed pattern of Chinese economic transition, as a gradual, evolutionary movement, ultimately rests on understanding a set of relationships among elites where the conservatives were in a stronger political position than the reformers. China's divergence from the Eastern European experience of economic reform cannot, therefore, be fully explained by recourse to arguments about differences in cultural values and Chinese preferences for collectivism and long-term social stability. While such factors may indeed need to be considered carefully, the observed path dependency in China's transition was, as Guo (2006) notes, also influenced by political conflict and compromise among China's ruling elite.

Another study relevant to our concerns here is Bell & Feng's (2013) research on the People's Bank of China (PBC) in the post-1978 reform period. They show how the rise of the PBC depended heavily on political patronage, as well as on perceptions that its managers had highly developed professional competencies. Based on interviews with key actors, they show how their informants skilfully negotiated a complex political situation. By carefully building alliances they were able to navigate the PBC through 'economic crisis, changing historical contexts, wider constellations of political power (especially within the party leadership), changes in public policy and changing ideational as well as structural contexts' (Bell & Feng 2013, p. 16). They note that their participants were active agents who were 'interpretive', seeking to 'make sense' of their world while attempting to 'forge new patterns of change by utilizing ideational resources and wider contexts' (Bell & Feng, 2013, p. 16). In their analysis, Bell and Feng (2013) resist the 'sticky', or path-dependent, explanations that are used in many institutional perspectives, arguing instead for an 'agent-centred' version of historical institutionalism which allows for at least some organizational change, to be accounted for by human action.

Fundamentally, historical institutionalists argue that, at their base level, institutions and organizations are the outcome of historical struggles for political power. The explanatory emphasis is on developing a 'power-political view of institutions where the continuity of institutions may be understood through their distributional effects and increasing returns to power' (Mahoney & Thelen, 2010, p. 7). Once a power elite has been established, then radical change is difficult. Understanding the path-dependent appearance of China's transition, in both economy and organization, means giving due regard to the influence of the state and the legacy of the institutions of the command economy (P. H. Nolan, 1995). That said, Bell and Feng's (2013) research shows that it is also possible to observe some examples of organizational change which have emerged from the strategies and practices adopted by individual executives and managers, thus creating a space for understanding the role of 'embedded' human agency. In the following section, we will discuss the emergence of a new critique of institutionalist perspectives, especially the North American sociological and organizational varieties, which seeks to emphasize even further the role of power and power relations in accounting for change and stability. This perspective has important implications for understanding the organizational and management practices of Western bankers in China, the core focus of this study.

Conceptions of power in organizational and institutional analysis

New institutionalism, especially as it has developed in its sociological, historical and organizational variants, assumes that organizational actors are influenced by rationalized 'myths', institutional 'logics' and 'legitimacy seeking' (Morgan et al., 2014). One of the key concerns of new institutionalism has been to investigate processes that lead to *isomorphism* (or similarity) in both the behaviour of managers and the organizational forms and institutions in which they are embedded. The general focus of this framework has been on tracing processes of path dependency and institutional stability, which has led some to question how organizational *change* might actually be accounted for. As Morgan et al. (2014, p. 934) note, in order to account for change, institutionalists needed to develop new concepts such as 'institutional entrepreneurship', 'institutional work', 'embedded agency' and 'inhabited institutions' (Lawrence, Leca & Zilber, 2013; Lawrence, Suddaby & Leca, 2011). However, while such concepts have been useful additions to addressing the so-called 'problem of change' in institutional thinking, some believe that a more fundamental difficulty with the perspective is its lack of engagement with examining the processes of power in institutional and organizational settings (Clegg, 1989; Munir, 2015; Willmott, 2015). We hope to contribute to the debate on such thinking in more concrete terms in later chapters.

In the following sections, we do not attempt a comprehensive examination of all the literature concerned with theories of power (see Clegg (1989) for a broader review). What we aim to do is to evaluate those elements which are most suitable for understanding the empirical focus of this particular study. As a starting point, we will outline Lukes's (1974) much-cited 'three-dimensional model' of power. Lukes's model initially distinguishes between the 'first' and 'second' dimensions of power. The first dimension refers to 'overt' acts of power, assumed to be based on an actor's will. For example, Dahl (1957, p. 202) defines power as the quantifiable decision-making which occurs when 'A has power over B to the extent that he can get B to do something that B would not otherwise do'. The second dimension of power identified by Lukes is concerned with its 'covert' qualities – that is, with the ability of certain groups to determine what is actually important in the decision-making processes in the first place (Bachrach & Baratz, 1962). Lukes's personal contribution was to extend the debates by drawing attention to the way in which power might be 'latent'. That is, that it may be recognised by its ability to 'implant in people's minds interests that are contrary to their own good' (Sadan, 1997, p. 37). This 'third' dimension of power is difficult to identify, not least because it rests on a normative observation made by a removed third party who ostensibly knows what is 'good' for a particular group and, furthermore, classifies that group as having no knowledge of the ways in which it is being manipulated. Nevertheless, Lukes argues convincingly that a comprehensive study of power must examine not just open decision-making (Dahl's (1957) 'overt' face), and non-decisions (Bachrach & Baratz's (1962) 'covert' face), but also the broader political agenda and historical context within which interests emerge and influence the ideas of less powerful groups, sometimes to their own detriment (Sadan, 1997).

Developing some of these ideas, Clegg (1989), draws on the work of Foucault (1980) to argue that power also has 'distributed' qualities and should not be thought of as a specific 'force', clearly located in discrete individuals or organizations. For Clegg (1989), power should be viewed as a circular process which flows through different channels or 'circuits', each with its own set of social relations. In brief, he argues that what happens in organizations and institutions is not dependent on the nature of power in just one circuit, but, rather, on how power moves between circuits and, subsequently, where opportunities for resistance may emerge.

Clegg's model has been used in numerous empirical studies of SOEs in China; however, its application by Child and Lu (1990) to industrial decision-making in the 1980s is particularly interesting. They show that power does indeed 'circulate' around China's industrial system, through local administrative bodies, professionalized managers and government policy-makers. The underdevelopment of both bureaucratic and market modes of economic action in the mid-1980s created a series of *negotiated dependency relations* which were, in turn, embedded in both local obligations and national policy expectations. In relation to understanding institutional and organizational change, this perspective draws attention to the dynamic, circular nature of power where outcomes are not always predictable or readily 'explained' by recourse to mainstream cultural or institutional perspectives.

Finally, it is not possible to discuss the concept of power without further reference to the influential work of Michel Foucault (1926–1984) (Foucault 1977, 1980). In one sense, Foucault does not, like Lukes and Clegg, have a clearly identifiable system of power. Indeed, his views on power change over the course of his writings (Gane, 2013; Walzer, 1986). He is not concerned with defining a 'final truth' because, he argues, meaning is distributed across societies and institutions, rather than centred in an 'autonomous' individual subject (Gane, 2013). In brief, his analysis of the historical records of particular institutions, such as prisons and mental asylums, demonstrated that the development and implementation of new technologies (such as putting prisoners under surveillance through new forms of prison design) led to forms of 'disciplinary' power which operated not just through physical punishment, but through mechanisms of hierarchical observation, judgements about 'normality', and processes of 'scientific' examination of what is allegedly 'normal' (Foucault, 1977). Of particular relevance to this study is his view that the operation of power is not confined to specific spheres of political life, but may manifest through the discourses and routine practices of everyday life, a theme that will be developed in later empirical chapters.

Foucault's ideas on power have been adapted by some scholars interested in studying Chinese institutions and organizations, especially those working within anthropological traditions. An example is Mayfair Yang's (1994) research on the changing use of *guanxi* practice, or *guanxi xue*, in business and politics during the post-1978 reform period. Yang shows that the nature of relationship-building and gift exchange, far from being a 'timeless' immutable feature of Chinese culture, changed over time based on the political and institutional context. For example, she notes that during the Maoist period in China (1946–1976) there was a widely held view among the political elite that 'traditional' cultural practices (such as *guanxi* and *guanxi xue*) were 'feudal' and a hindrance to Chinese self-transformation (Yang, 1994). Drawing on Foucault, Yang argues that this period was based on an ideology which equated 'rational knowledge with emancipation and progress' as well as the political suppression of certain cultural 'preferences' that were viewed by the elites as retrograde (Yang, 1994, p. 39). Yang's own ethnographic study demonstrates that *guanxi xue* rapidly re-emerged during the post-1978 reform period, serving, in part, as a mode of opposition to new lines of official and bureaucratic power. By applying an historical analysis, Yang argues that the nature of power during this period bore similarities to the power systems identified by Foucault in the West, specifically the ever-encroaching power of bureaucratic administration over people's daily lives. Her explanation of the re-emergence of *guanxi xue* is that it served as a form of informal resistance to the 'totalizing' discourse of state power which attempted to construct new norms of what was 'right' and 'wrong' in Chinese society.

That said, Yang (1994, p. 35) also notes that the Chinese administration 'not only destroyed some aspects of Chinese tradition but also appropriated and strengthened others, with the result that the arrangement of power in China today, however novel, still has a very familiar Chinese flavour'. She observes that elements of power that did not concern Foucault, especially the Chinese state's continuing recourse to physical punishment and the enduring personal power of elites, remain important features in the field of power as it operates in China today. In other words, the 'first' (overt) and 'second' (covert) dimensions of power, as identified by Lukes (1974), are still relevant in the Chinese case. In this particular study, the groups investigated, Western and Chinese bankers, are not respectively 'powerless' in the conventional sense, but they are, as will be demonstrated in the following chapters, dependent on each other for different resources. This study will explore the modes of discourse and communication adopted by each group as they negotiate the complex field of power in the Chinese banking sector. However, it will also investigate the field of political decision-making (the overt 'first' dimension) and the development of values and beliefs (the covert 'second' dimension). By doing so, it is possible to identify a range of diverse strategies and practices used by participants, noting how they may constitute forms of resistance to top-down policies aimed at initiating institutional and organizational change (Clegg, 1989; Giddens, 1984).

Conclusion

This chapter has introduced the fundamental *theoretical* debates that will underpin arguments developed in later empirical chapters. It has outlined the widespread interest in studying cultural values and capitalist development, and it has demonstrated the important contributions made by *institutional* perspectives, especially as they relate to debates around convergence and divergence in social and economic action. Institutionalism itself takes a number of forms, each foregrounding different explanatory concepts and using evidence drawn from different levels of analysis. While a number of insights can be drawn from these perspectives, we have also seen that both cultural and institutional analysis can be developed further by considering in more detail the explanatory potential of the concept of power. Certainly, 'power', 'culture' and 'institution' are complex terms which are defined in different ways by different theorists. The reason for discussing the aspects of power highlighted above is that they are the most pragmatically useful for understanding the problems which this book seeks to investigate and the themes that eventually emerged from the data. The next chapter will introduce some more specific details about the Chinese banking sector and the role and influence of Western banks within that field. In order to do this, the chapter will draw on comparative business systems approaches which also attempt to integrate the core concepts introduced here, namely culture, institutions and power relations (Whitley, 1999; Redding, 2005).

Note

1 A global regulatory framework for evaluating bank capital adequacy and stress testing. This will be discussed in more detail in Chapter 5.

3 The variety of business systems in China's banking sector

China's banking sector consists of a number of different kinds of institutions and, as a consequence, the sector itself is composed of diverse business systems. The first part of this chapter will discuss these systems and the second will contextualize the role of Western bankers in each different system. To do this, we will use a comparative business approach (Boisot & Child, 1996; Redding, 2005; Whitley, 1992, 1999). This perspective allows researchers the space to develop studies which use interpretive methods to build 'thick descriptions' of relevant case studies (Geertz, 1973). As noted in Chapters 1 and 2, in order to achieve new insights into the complex processes which influence cultural values, institutional change and power relations in international business and management, it is necessary to investigate situational complexity. Comparative business systems approaches provide conceptual frameworks which have the scope and flexibility to achieve this aim and can thus deepen our understanding of the Chinese banking sector.

The Chinese banking sector

Over the last 15 years, China's state-owned banks (SOBs) have moved from being technically 'insolvent' to taking the lead in the global banking profitability rankings.

In fact, a recent account argued that the main value added in the Chinese economy was coming from the financial sector. According to a report released in June 2016 by the McKinsey Global Institute (MGI), a think-tank:

> over four-fifths of all 'economic profits' (which take into account the cost of capital) generated in China come from one industry: finance. And that is not the result of the brilliance of China's bankers, but rather of state-run banks being guaranteed profits by the regulatory system.
>
> ('Sleepy Giant', 2016)

As can be seen in Table 3.1, since the start of the financial crisis in 2008, China's 'big four' SOBs have taken at least the top two positions and, in 2013, occupied the top four places. Löchel and Li (2011, p. 5) cite data from *The Banker* (2010)

Table 3.1 Global top ten banks by pre-tax profit 2007–2013

2007			*2008*		
Bank	*Country*	*US$ million*	*Bank*	*Country*	*US$ million*
1 Bank of America	USA	31,973	**1 ICBC**	**China**	**21,270**
2 Citigroup	USA	29,639	**2 CCB**	**China**	**17,520**
3 HSBC Holdings	UK	22,086	3 Banco Santander	Spain	15,825
4 JP Morgan Chase	USA	19,886	**4 BOC**	**China**	**12,620**
5 Royal Bank of Scotland	UK	18,033	5 BBVA	Spain	9,640
6 Crédit Agricole	France	14,060	6 HSBC Holdings	UK	9, 307
7 Barclays Bank	UK	14,009	7 Barclays Bank	UK	8,859
8 BNP Paribas	France	13,921	**8 ABC**	**China**	**7,659**
9 Mitsubishi UFJ Financial Group	Japan	12,824	9 UniCredit	Italy	6,952
10 Wells Fargo	USA	12,745	10 Royal Bank of Canada	Canada	6,077
2010			*2013*		
Bank	*Country*	*US$ million*	*Bank*	*Country*	*US$ million*
1 ICBC	**China**	**32,528**	**1 ICBC**	**China**	**55,479**
2 CCB	**China**	**26,448**	**2 CCB**	**China**	**45,854**
3 JP Morgan Chase	USA	24,859	**3 ABC**	**China**	**35,098**
4 BOC	**China**	**21,463**	**4 BOC**	**China**	**34,870**
5 HSBC Holdings	UK	19,037	5 Wells Fargo	USA	32,283
6 Wells Fargo	USA	18,700	6 JP Morgan Chase	USA	25,914
7 ABC	**China**	**18,230**	7 HSBC Holdings	UK	22,565
8 BNP Paribas	France	17,406	8 Citigroup	USA	19,656
9 Banco Santander	Spain	16079	9 Bank of America	USA	16,181
10 Goldman Sachs	USA	12,892	10 Mitsubishi UFJ Financial Group	Japan	14,653

Adapted from: Alexander (2013); Löchel & Li (2011).

which shows that 101 Chinese banks were included in the *Top 1000 World Banks* in 2010 and that they collectively contributed 21% of global banking profits. Indeed, some of the SOBs saw the financial crisis of 2008 as an opportunity to begin serious overseas expansion – for example, ICBC's purchase of 20% of Standard Bank Group, the largest bank in Africa (Löchel & Li, 2011). Commentators note that the success of the SOBs stems from their receipt of large capital injections from the state, asset carve-outs, reforms to ownership structure, the introduction of foreign minority shareholders with seats on the board, and efforts to adopt 'best practices' approaches to risk management and corporate governance (Cousin, 2011; Löchel & Li, 2011).

However, beyond the very obvious successes of the SOBs in the global profit rankings, it is important to recognize that the Chinese banking sector, like China itself, is extremely large, diverse and highly complex. At the end of 2013, China had 31 provinces, 656 cities, eight recognized dialects of Mandarin (and 80 other Chinese dialects) (China Statistical Yearbook, 2014). Moreover, the central and regional governments are often at odds in terms of policy and law enforcement. As Shih (2008) notes, political and geographical factions in the field of finance are particularly rife and the enforcement of commercial and banking laws remains highly capricious. During 2011, the banking system consisted of approximately 3,800 institutions with close to 3.2 million employees (CBRC, 2012). Table 3.2 lists the principal types of institutions in the sector, ranked by asset scale. In brief, China's size and diversity means that it is not possible to describe a 'national' market for many products, including financial ones (Boisot & Child, 1996; Warner, 2013; Whitley, 1992; Witt, 2012).

The variety of different institutions, ownership structures and product niches in the banking sector means there are also different kinds of business systems in place.

Table 3.2 Main types of institutions in Chinese banking sector at the end of 2011

Types of institution
State-owned commercial banks (SCBs)
47% of total banking assets
The 'big four', namely the Bank of China (BOC), Industrial and Commercial Bank of China (ICBC), China Construction Bank (CCB), Agricultural Bank of China (ABC)
Joint-stock commercial banks (JSCBs)
16% of total banking assets
Twelve in total at the time of the study; examples include the Bank of Communications (BoCom), China Everbright Bank, Guangdong Development Bank and Shanghai Pudong Development Bank
Rural credit co-operatives (and other SME rural financial institutions)
15% of total assets
2,265 in total
Policy banks and China Development Bank
12% of total assets
City commercial banks and urban credit co-operatives
8% of total assets
144 in total
Locally incorporated foreign banking institutions (in development)
2% of total assets
40 in total

Source: CBRC (2012).

As such, we would expect day-to-day managerial practices to vary according to the particular business system in which any given bank is placed. In relation to the concerns of this study, it is possible to identify *five* different banking systems in China (Cousin, 2011). First, there is the *state-owned business system* which consists of the SOBs and the joint-stock commercial banks (JSCBs). In these banks, there is clear evidence of foreign investment and related activities, such as technical assistance projects and the use of international advisors and consultants. Second is the *local corporate system*, which largely consists of the city commercial banks which were set up in the post-1978 reform period. These are principally urban-based units, under the administration of local government. As with the SOBs, there has been notable foreign investment and related activity in this system. Third, there is the *rural credit co-operative* system, which provides financial services for farmers and those engaged in other agricultural activities. In almost all cases, institutions in this system conform to co-operative ownership forms. Fourth, there is the *foreign locally incorporated system*, which consists of wholly owned foreign banks who are attempting to flourish independently (these were fully established in 2013, but were under development during the period of this study). Fifth, there is the *shadow banking system* which includes informal lenders, such as pawnbrokers and underground banks, as well as trust companies that make loans but do not collect deposits. This research draws mainly on information gathered from participants involved with banks based in the *state-owned, local corporate* and *foreign locally incorporated* systems. Table 3.3 shows the main Western investments in these banks during the fieldwork phase of this research.[1]

Understanding business systems in China's banking sector

The key characteristics of the state-owned, local corporate and foreign locally incorporated business systems will be outlined below using Redding's (2005) model of comparative business systems in East Asia. This model provides an important set of organizing concepts, supplementing and incorporating the insights provided by the institutional, cultural and power-relations perspectives outlined in Chapter 2. Redding's (2005) framework consists of three interlinked levels of analysis. At the base level, is the realm of 'meaning', which, following Berger and Luckmann (1966), is broadly defined as the 'social construction of reality'. In the intermediary position is the realm of 'order', which focuses on the influence of three forms of capital: financial, human and social. At the top of the model, Redding places different forms of 'firm coordination', including ownership structures, networks and management. The system in its entirety is intertwined with 'material logics' (the impact of costs and technologies) and 'ideational logics' (the development of ideas, norms and values). These concepts were discussed in detail in Chapter 2. Redding does not develop a detailed account of how power might operate in institutions and organizations, but he does make important points about how

Table 3.3 Key Western investments in China's SOBs, JSCBs and CCBs in 2010

Chinese bank	*Western investor*	*Stake (as a percentage)*
Industrial and Commercial Bank of China	Goldman Sachs Group American Express Allianz Investments	3% 0.4% 2%
China Construction Bank Corporation	Bank of America Fullerton Financial Holdings	10.2% 5.6%
Bank of Communications	Hong Kong and Shanghai Banking Corporation (HSBC)	18.6%
Shanghai Pudong Development Bank	Citibank Overseas Investment Corporation	2.7%
Hua Xia Bank	Deutsche Bank	11.3%
Bank of Beijing	ING Bank International Finance Corporation	16.1% 4%
Bank of Shanghai	HSBC International Finance Corporation	8% 3%
Bank of Tianjin	Australia and New Zealand Banking Group Limited	18%
Bank of Nanjing	BNP Paribas	12.7%
Bank of Guanzhou	Bank of Nova Scotia	19.9%
Bank of Hangzhou	Commonwealth Bank of Australia	20%
Qilu Bank	Commonwealth Bank of Australia	19.9%
China Bohai Bank	Standard Chartered Bank	19.9%
Bank of Qingdao	Rothschilds Continuation Holdings AG	5%
Nanchong City Commercial Bank	Deutsche Investitions-und Entwicklungsgeselleschaft (DEG)	10%
Shanghai Rural Commercial Bank	Australia and New Zealand Banking Group Limited	20%
Guangdong Development Bank (Guangfa Bank)	Citigroup Inc IBM Credit LLC	20% 5%
Tianjin Binhai Rural Commercial Bank	International Finance Corporation	10.6%
Hangzhou United Bank	Rabobank International Finance Corporation	9.9% 5%
Xiamen International Bank	Sino-US JV Financial group	5%
Xi'an City Commercial Bank	Bank of Nova Scotia	14.8%

Adapted from: KPMG Huanzhen (2011).

cultural understandings of organizational rationales, authority relationships and state decision-making might impact on management practices. In this chapter, we will use the model to introduce specific contextual information and important explanatory concepts, both of which will inform the empirical data presented later in the study.

Culture and meaning: extending the 'values' definition

Redding (2005) adopts a definition of culture which fully embraces the socially constructed 'meanings' that we attach to the world around us. This contrasts with the mainstream orthodoxy in ICCM, which, as noted in Chapter 2, tends to adopt a narrow definition of culture focused solely on societal differences in values. For Redding (2005), one of the main problems with contemporary research on culture is that, for methodological reasons, it has attempted to separate 'cultural values' from 'context', a move which stems, in large part, from the dominance of the positivist epistemological paradigm in North American business schools. Redding (2005) argues that there is now a real need to move towards more holistic investigations of culture as *meaning* (Ragin, 1987; Geertz, 1973), where the importance of interest groups, the influence of history and the role of the state are not 'factored out' in the pursuit of highly decontextualized results which answer extremely narrow questions (see also Child, 2009). Following Geertz (1973), he notes that, culture is 'a system of construable signs and symbols, interwoven with the world of action, not directly causing the formation of institutions, behaviours or processes but as the context within which those institutions can be intelligently and "thickly" described' (Redding 2005, p. 129). In brief, 'culture' is about what things mean to people. To understand meaning involves embracing context, not factoring it out as inconvenient 'noise'. In his model of comparative business systems, he is especially interested in analyzing how meaning influences the interpretation and allocation of authority, the definition of identity and belonging, as well as the development of interpersonal trust and the formation of institutions. In the following sections we will discuss these ideas in relation to the first three elements of his model: rationale, identity and authority.

Rationale

'Rationale' relates to the way societies conceptualize both what the suitable objectives, or 'ends', of economic action should be, as well as identifying the appropriate tools or 'means' for achieving those ends (Witt, 2006; Redding & Witt, 2007). Applying this idea specifically to China's SOBs and JSCBs, it is important to note that, as well as being driven by the rationale, or goal, of profitability, these banks are also given important policy objectives by the government which are aimed at furthering China's economic development and re-establishing China as a significant global economic force. Banking is central to ensuring China's economic future and, as such, the state retains majority ownership in all key institutions. The strategic importance of banks means that the SOBs are closely monitored by the State-owned Assets and Supervision Administration Commission (SASAC), which also supervises other sectors of the economy that are important to national and economic security, such as telecommunications and energy (Cousin, 2011). While SOBs have been put under some pressure to reform and become more market-orientated, they remain heavily influenced by state-level policy decision-making. For example, in 2009, when the global banking crisis was at its most intense, the banks were instructed to take a 'soft' approach to their debtors, and to roll over loans in a way reminiscent of the policies of the Mao era (1949–1976) ('Too big to hail', 2013). During this period, huge loans were made to the SOEs, creating highly problematic non-performing loans (NPLs) and a complacent management cadre who were effectively unaccountable for their decisions (this policy is discussed in more detail in Chapter 4). In brief, the fundamental *rationale* underlying the management and regulation of the SOBs and JSCBs in China differs somewhat from those found in banks in the USA and the UK. While it is fair to say that a number of Western banks have also received considerable state support over recent years, Chinese regulators still place relatively more emphasis on the role of banks in promoting China's economic growth, rather than simply as vehicles for the pursuit of profit. As later chapters will show, this basic difference in beliefs about the underlying *objectives* of banks impacts on interactions between Chinese and Western managers, creating organizational practices that may be based on conflict, prevarication, and sometimes even sabotage.

Identity

Another important feature of 'culture' relates to the construction of identity in any given society (Redding, 2005). As noted in Chapter 2, much research in ICCM investigates culture and identity by drawing on the work of Hofstede (2001), a framework which seeks to sub-divide the construct of identity into discrete, measurable items. In this section, we will provide further detail on Hofstede's work and summarize critiques of his conceptualization and measurement of culture (Jack & Westwood, 2009; McSweeney, 2002; Redding, 2005). We will also show how the relationship between culture and identity remains important for analyzing authority relations and work values, especially for research concerned with cross-national comparison.

Hofstede and his colleagues (Hofstede & Bond, 1988; Hofstede, 2001) originally identified *five* dimensions of cultural difference in work values and identities, namely: (i) power distance (which relates to feelings about the acceptable degree of supervisory control in the workplace), (ii) uncertainty avoidance (the degree to which people avoid the unknown to manage stress), (iii) individualism (the importance placed on the individual as opposed to the group), (iv) masculinity (the relative importance of earning and achievement versus cooperation and collaborative organizational atmospheres), and (v) long-term and short-term orientations (the importance attached to the future as opposed to the past, originally labelled as 'Confucian dynamism').[2] In 2011, a sixth dimension, 'indulgence orientation', was also included (the pursuit of personal satisfaction through leisure, sex and consumption) (Hofstede, 2011). In addition to Hofstede's model, there are numerous other approaches based on the quantitative measurement of psychological dimensions related to culture, values and identity (Triandis, 2004; Hampden-Turner & Trompenaars, 1993; House et al., 2004).

While tremendously appealing to many researchers in international management, these models have not been without their critics. Javidan, et al. (2006), for example, argue that, at a very fundamental level, there is clearly more to culture than values. They propose a model which distinguishes between subjective values and more manifest 'practices', which they loosely define as the actual ways people go about dealing with their collective challenges. They also differentiate between values and practices which relate to work (organizational cultures) and those relating to wider society (societal cultures). However, as Earley (2006) note, while Javidan et al. (2006) and Hofstede (2006) may disagree over the relative merit of using either values or practices to define culture, both still rest on narrow, decontextualized, conceptualizations of the concept. They are, in many ways, ideologically similar, in that the emphasis is still placed on defining culture in such a way that it can then be measured using quantitative questionnaires based on Likert scales, administered to large samples, and the results analyzed using conventional statistical analysis (Smith, 2006; McSweeney, 2002). There are fierce debates about the problems of using this kind of methodology to study culture and identity. For example, Smith (2006) argues that these techniques create a false impression of cultural uniformity, negating the existence of subcultures and hybrid identities. Moreover, it has real difficulty in capturing the relationship between culture and other forms of social and political influence (Jack & Westwood, 2009; McSweeney, 2002; Redding, 2005). McSweeney (2002) also asks the important question of whether or not it really makes sense to claim that a nation, as such, can have a culture given that territorial borders of modern nation-states can and do shift. Others have argued that Hofstede's model remains central to ICCM principally because it offers a fairly 'easy' way to design and carry out a research study. There is considerable career pressure on academics to publish copious amounts of work over relatively short periods of time, and 'dimensional' research studies, based on pre-existing definitions and measures, can be completed in relatively short periods (as compared with in-depth ethnographies, for example) (Jack & Westwood, 2009; Redding, 2005).

All that said, as noted in Chapter 2, Hofstede's individualism-collectivism dimension continues to occupy the mainstream of ICCM research. Countless studies have investigated how this dimension might influence management practices ranging from recruitment and retention through to supply chain management, strategy decision-making, marketing techniques, and accounting procedures (see Warner, 2014a, for a review). While there is considerable debate about how best to study subjective factors such as identity and cultural values, it is fair to say that diversity both *within* and *between* Asian and Western identities do appear to have some influence on the operation of national business systems (Redding, 2005; Redding & Witt, 2007). Pre-existing social preferences, however they are conceptualized and measured, are embedded in interpersonal ties and networks that have an enduring influence on institutional and organizational development (Geertz, 1973; Granovetter, 1985). In the study, we will focus on the importance of culture and identity issues in relationships of trust and dependence, as well as network allegiances and modes of conformity (Chapters 5, 6 and 7). We will also examine the way in which participants understand and construct identity in relation both to self and to other. The aim will be to investigate how local understandings of culture are used to negotiate an organizational field which is defined not just by perceived cultural 'difference' but also by differential access to resources and unstable power relations.

Authority

Culture and meaning also influence local understandings of 'authority'. This operates in two ways in Redding's model. On one level, it refers to social norms in relation to paternalism and meritocracy. On another, it is concerned with how power is defined, legitimized and executed. In some ways, the first level is captured in discussions of identity (outlined above). It may relate to what Hofstede (2001) refers to as 'power-distance', where the emphasis may be on hierarchical respect for age seniority, length of service and educational attainment. In Chapter 7 of this book, there is some indication that problems emerge when Western expatriates, who may have been posted on an overseas assignment because they possess certain technical competencies, are perceived as being too junior or inexperienced to take on a role which involves engagement with a more senior Chinese partner. Western banks who dedicate the time and money to send more senior individuals are perceived by their Chinese partners as more 'sensitive' to Chinese culture. Javidan et al. (2006) also emphasize that 'power distance' can refer to the degree to which members of a group *expect* power to be distributed equally. In other words, social systems based on meritocratic reward in the workplace are not considered to be universally desirable, and expectations of equality and access to power vary accordingly. Working with national-level data, they note that countries with high power-distance scores usually have relatively unequal power distribution within their societies. These countries, which include China, tend to be more stratified economically, socially and politically. Moreover, those in positions of authority, be they politicians or business leaders, expect, and often receive, high levels of obedience from their subordinates. Their decision-making tends to be hierarchical, with limited emphasis on communication and consultation (Javidan et al., 2006). There are many studies which link high levels of power distance in China to its Confucian traditions, especially the tendency for workplace relationships to be driven by strong paternalistic, vertical linkages between employees and managers (Rowley, Benson & Warner, 2004; Warner, 2010; Zhu, Warner & Rowley, 2007). However, it is also important to emphasize that the need to establish hierarchical relationships may also be partly attributed to weaknesses in the institutional and legal frameworks in China (Gold, Guthrie & Wank, 2002). Dysfunctional institutions create a need to access the security and opportunities provided through establishing connections with networks of powerful individuals (Warner, 2014a; Yang, 1994).

The second way in which Redding (2005) discusses authority relates to varying definitions and interpretations of power, some of which were introduced in Chapter 2. As Warner (2010) notes, the growing literature on the identification of Confucian principles in management practices in China cannot be explained simply through 'cultural differences'. The terms must be contextualized against the backdrop of the current popular discourse on Confucianism in China, which coexists with Sino-Marxism and the CCP's adoption of the concept of the 'harmonious society' to legitimate its current political agenda. In other words, it is important to foreground how institutional and political influences may shape 'traditional' elements of Chinese culture. These themes are discussed in further detail in Chapter 4, where we introduce debates about the causes and consequences of a growing nationalist discourse in China based on a particular interpretation of past historical events (Callahan, 2012; Wang, 2014). Indeed, the CCP itself needs to be understood as a formal hierarchical structure within Chinese society and the 'overt' power of the state manifests itself plainly in China's SOE business system (Bell & Feng, 2013; Redding & Witt, 2007).

Order and institutions

In Redding's (2005) model, the domain of culture and meaning generates the rules which define institutional order in a given society. The 'realm of order' can range from individualized social norms such as dress codes and table manners (Elias & Jephcott, 1978; Bourdieu, 1984), through to large-scale macro-level rules, such as the codified statutes of a legal system (Redding & Witt, 2007). Redding also makes a distinction between formal (proximate) institutions and informal (background) influences which include culture and meaning. While acknowledging that there will necessarily be some 'slippage' between the influences of formal and informal institutions, he argues that the elements that are most important for understanding changes in business systems will be those which influence the key resources on which businesses depend. These include: (i) 'capital', defined as 'the realm of assets such as money, land, technology, [and includes] … institutions such as banks, accounting systems, financial regulations and commercial laws' (Redding & Witt, 2007, p. 22); (ii) 'human capital', which refers to the knowledge and skills of a population that are developed through education systems, vocational training provision and opportunities in the labour market; and (iii) 'social capital' which, in this context, refers to the various mechanisms which may influence both individual and institutional trust (Putnam, 1995).

Capital

Within the various business systems identified above (SOB, local corporate, foreign locally incorporated, etc.), sources of financial capital differ. This in itself has consequences for understanding processes of institutional change. As noted earlier, because of their strategic importance, the large SOBs remain majority owned by the central government (via the investment vehicle, Central Huijin Ltd, an arm of the sovereign wealth fund, the China Investment Corporation) (Cousin, 2011). Consequently, the state retains control, via supervisory committees, of the majority of strategic decisions, including those related to the approval of major loans. For example, in 2013, around 75% of SOB loans were, in fact, extended to other Chinese SOEs on 'soft' repayment terms which were most certainly open to renegotiation in difficult times (Tsai, 2015). On the other hand, China's SMEs, which generate around 60% of China's GDP, continue to have very little access to capital from the SOBs. In 2013, for example, they received only 23% of their financing from this source (Tsai, 2015). Indeed, at the time of writing, there is only one privately owned bank in China of any significance, the Minsheng Bank, and although this particular institution does concentrate on SME funding, most private enterprises in China still find themselves relying on loans from non-banking financial institutions. These may include sources such as credit-guarantee companies, pawnbrokers and micro-finance companies, as well as informal 'underground' shadow banks (Tsai, 2007, 2015). In brief, the formal banking sector in China continues to be largely dominated by the pattern of SOBs lending to state-owned enterprises, a model which has changed very little throughout the reform period (Nolan, 2009). Some Chinese policy-makers are pressing hard to improve the funding opportunities for SMEs, but the shadow banking system looks set to dominate this sector for the foreseeable future (Jacob & Rabinovitch, 2011). As discussed in Chapter 1, one of the fundamental reasons for allowing foreign bank entry into China in the first place was, ostensibly, to create greater competition within the domestic sector and, as a consequence, to provide a more comprehensive range of financial facilities to Chinese businesses as a whole, especially to SMEs. However, with a market share of less than 2% (CBRC, 2014), the lowest share of a national banking sector held by foreign banks in any of the larger emerging economies, this objective has not been met ('China wall hit', 2012; Claessens & Horen, 2014). As will be discussed in Chapter 5, the perceived threat of foreign banks to China's economic security, associated with formal and informal obstruction to their business development at the organizational level, means that full competition in China's banking sector is an unlikely outcome for the foreseeable future. To appreciate the rationale underlying China's ambivalent approach to market 'competition' requires a nuanced understanding of the historical and cultural context in which China's modern banking sector emerged. This will be the subject of Chapter 4 and later empirical chapters.

Human capital

The skills and talents of employees in China's banking sector vary quite considerably. There is some evidence that managers in the SOBs are now being recruited in a more competitive manner, with some degree of focus on their professional background and educational attainments (Cousin, 2011). Nevertheless, appointments at director level in the SOBs remains under the direction of the CCP and the SASAC. As such, it is crucial for executives to be actively involved with party matters in order to gain high-level promotions. The performance incentives of executives are, therefore, not entirely market-driven and so their decision-making may also be based on achieving political objectives. Profit maximization will not always be their primary goal (Cousin, 2011). At the level of middle management, addressing inadequacies in human capital was another reason for allowing foreign bank entry to the sector. Much was made of the possibility of 'knowledge transfer' in joint ventures and of the importance of Western 'expertise' in training bank staff at all levels (see the discussion of the IMF technical assistance projects in Chapter 6). There have been numerous case studies of such projects – for example, Citi's investment in the Guangdong Bank and Newbridge's investment in Pudong Development Bank (Ferri, 2009; Leigh & Podpiera, 2006) – and Chapter 6 will chart the experiences of both foreign and domestic managers in attempting to improve human capital in the sector. It will show how differing rationales, a lack of trust, and shifting power dynamics have a strong influence on knowledge transfer processes.

Social capital

Social capital can be defined as the degree of trust in a society. Trust can operate at two different, but inter-related, levels (Redding & Witt, 2007). First, there is the nature of trust between individuals, and, second, there is the level of trust in the institutional context itself (Putnam, 1995). In China, institutional trust, which includes public confidence in the fairness and integrity of legal and regulatory systems, remains relatively low (Transparency International, 2010). As indicated earlier, partly as a consequence of this general lack of trust in institutions, reliance on extensive interpersonal networks (*guanxi*) may become magnified (Luo, 2008; Yang, 1994). Some have argued that a heavy reliance on *guanxi*, especially when the network includes friends and family who have known each other for many years, may create a situation where network members find it increasingly difficult to trust *strangers* (a phenomenon which is, of course, not confined solely to Chinese social networks) (Ermisch & Gambetta, 2010; Fukuyama, 1995). In relation to this book, Chapter 6 shows that *guanxi* networks are still important in loan decisions and corporate governance mechanisms, leading to situations where standardised risk-assessment procedures are simply ignored. Moreover, as we will show in Chapter 7, Western bankers perceive an enduring need to establish *guanxi* networks to advance their own interests, often achieving this through hiring the relatives of influential political and business figures. This practice ultimately reinforces the status quo in recruitment practices and loan decision-making in China's banking organizations, rather than effecting any significant change.

Business systems and co-ordination

The last element of Redding's (2005) model focuses on the forms of co-ordination which may tie together other elements of the system. These factors include types of ownership, networks *across* firm boundaries (inter-corporate networking), and the role of management activity *within* the firm.

Ownership

The SOBs are under the control of the State Council, the chief administrative authority of the PRC, via the SASAC. As discussed earlier, they remain majority owned by the state through government investment vehicles (Cousin, 2011). Between 2005 and 2010, the 'big four' SOBs went through IPOs in the international capital markets. They sold around 20% of their shares to foreign and commercial domestic shareholders (see Table 3.3), which diversified their ownership structure somewhat. The state does not retain such a strong hold on the JSCBs, but ownership is still largely in state hands, either directly, through the Ministry of Finance, or indirectly, through shares purchased by other SOEs (Cousin, 2011). Some JSCBs, such as Ping An Bank (formerly Shenzhen Development Bank) sought partnerships with Western banks (Cousin, 2011) but, as with the SOBs, maximum shareholding stakes for foreign investors are around 20% (Cousin, 2011). The city commercial banks are largely under the control of local governments who retain an average stake of 75% in each bank.

Many of the examples used in this book will refer to the role that foreign shareholders have played in changing the ownership structures and management practices of the SOBs, JSCBs and city commercial banks. The rationale for initially encouraging foreign shareholders (and the appointment of their associated executive representatives on the banks' Board of Directors) was that diverse ownership structures would help to resolve the conflicts of interest that may arise when 'principals' and 'agents' are one and the same entity (Clarke, 2011; Naughton, 2007). In other words, governance problems are thought to arise when the state is both owner (principal) and manager (agent). When the control of an organization remains in the hands of 'insiders', there are no robust independent entities that may challenge the decisions of internal interest groups and, as a consequence, moral hazard may develop (Clarke, 2011; Naughton, 2007). As will be discussed in more detail in Chapter 7, because the state remains heavily involved in the ownership, management and regulation of China's major banks, the principal–agent problem endures. However, to the extent that Chinese banks operate with different rationales, objectives and authority relationships to those commonly found in the West, the chapter will also consider whether or not the principal–agent 'problem' really *is* such a big a dilemma in the Chinese context (Clarke, 2011).

Networks

In China, strategic industries, such as finance and banking, remain closely networked to government at various levels (Cousin, 2011). Consequently, there is much less horizontal networking *between* firms than may be commonly found in the West. Witt and Redding (2013) note that in most Western economies horizontal firm networking is important for the acquisition of knowledge, capital, products and talent. However, in China, the legacy of state planning and the enduring control of the CCP over industry associations tends to militate against firm associations and other forms of independent co-ordinated action. This means that there is a stronger tendency towards *vertical* networking, a remnant of the planned economy when each sector was directly under the administration of a separate ministry (P. H. Nolan, 2001). In this study, the need to establish political connections manifests itself in the need to recruit individuals who are part of these networks (either through family connections or other close relationships). This is especially so among Western banks who are attempting to develop their own businesses in China, many of whom recruit Chinese employees whom they perceive to have strong political *guanxi* (Nolan, 2011). However, this form of personal networking is distinct from the study of horizontal firm networking as described by Podolny and Page (1998). Many of the micro-level practices which emerge through personal networking are best understood by reference to the debates on authority and identity introduced in the section on 'culture and meaning'.

Management

The final form of firm co-ordination identified by Redding (2005) relates to the role of managers who must organize the people, technologies and financial resources that are needed to ensure an organization's future (Redding & Witt, 2007). The issues of importance in this area range from the micro-level elements of human resource management, workplace learning and organizational adaptation, through to marketing, financial accounting and strategic planning. As noted above, most senior appointments in the state-owned banking sector are made on the basis of political commitment to the CCP, as well as on professional competency and experience (Brødsgaard, 2012). Senior managers must show a degree of sensitivity not just to profit-seeking but also to the strategic political and policy objectives aimed at improving China's economic development and international status. Expatriate managers, international advisors and other overseas technical experts must, therefore, interact with Chinese counterparts who are embedded in different organizational norms which are, in turn, nested in the political power structure of the

Chinese state. The extent to which the interactions between these two very different groups can initiate change in the banking sector will be a key theme in many of the following chapters.

Conclusion

In this chapter, we have suggested that China's banking sector is not in any way homogenous. While the 'big four' SOBs dominate the global profitability rankings, the sector itself is composed of different institutions which, in turn, create different kinds of business systems. This book concentrates on activities in the state-owned, local corporate and foreign locally incorporated systems. Redding's (2005) model offers an important schematic for understanding these different systems. As well as the concepts described and illustrated above, Redding also draws attention to the necessity of analyzing historical circumstance, the influence of the state and material and ideational factors. Clearly, the range of concepts and inter-relationships introduced so far highlights that this particular book will seek to describe and understand a *highly complex adaptive system* (Witt & Redding, 2013). In order to make sense of the multi-directional nature of interaction and influence between the different elements identified so far, it is, of course, important to situate the study within an historical analysis. China's treatment at the hands of foreign powers in the nineteenth century (and beyond) was severe and brutal, and these experiences continue to resonate in the public imagination today. This is particularly so given the kind of historiography encouraged by the CCP. Education policies have been developed which ensure that Chinese students are taught about history in such a way as to engender an acute sense of China's degradation at the hands of foreigners (Wang, 2014). In the next chapter, we will give an overview of the historical influence of foreign banking in China, showing how contemporary interpretations of these events colours perceptions of whether, and to what extent, Westerners can be trusted to support China's development today.

Notes

1 Further details of the sample are described in our Methodological Appendix, though to protect the anonymity of participants it will not be possible to name the banks where they were employed.
2 Although China was not included in the initial study of 40 countries conducted in 1967–1973, it was introduced into the analyses during the 1980s (Hofstede & Bond, 1988).

4 Western economic ideas and the historical development of Chinese banks

This chapter will map the evolution of the modern Chinese banking sector, focusing specifically on the impact that Western economic ideas and banking institutions had on its development. The events highlighted below have been selected because of their relevance to three important themes: (i) how they may have influenced contemporary perceptions of the utility of Western banking practices (what was referred to in Chapters 2 and 3 as 'ideational' influences); (ii) how these perceptions might have affected the current fortunes of Western banks in China; and (iii) how they help us to understand the complex roots of the distribution of power in the field of banking in China today.

The expansion and dominance of foreign banks in China 1840–1949

In the 1800s, the European colonial powers rapidly extended their global reach and their desire to increase trade with China intensified considerably (Peyrefitte, 2013). Britain, in particular, had a large trade deficit with China and attempted to establish greater access to the Chinese market in part through the now famous 'trade mission' led by Lord Macartney in 1792–93. As well as material objects (such as telescopes, clocks and barometers), the British sought to trade technology or 'useful knowledge', and Macartney recruited a range of 'technical experts', including scientific instrument makers, metallurgists and botanists to accompany him on the trip (Berg, 2006). He also took with him a letter from George III, addressed to the *Qianlong* Emperor, which stated that the mission's intentions were, ostensibly, to extend 'peaceful arts to the entire human race' and to share the 'knowledge of the world' (Hevia, 1995, p. 60). But the attempt to establish free trade links with China failed and Macartney was sent home with a message from the Emperor that 'we have never valued ingenious articles and have not the slightest need of your manufactures' (Lovell, 2012, p. 87). However, the British were not deterred. Despite fierce resistance from the Chinese authorities, they began shipping Indian opium to China in exchange for goods which were in high demand in Britain such as tea, porcelain and silk. Two separate Opium Wars (1840–42 and 1856–60) were fought between China and Britain over this practice, but, ultimately, Britain achieved victory and China was forced to open its southern ports to Western trade (Spence, 1990; Lovell, 2012).

With this enforced influx of foreign trade came the need for banking services. In the 1860s, Western banks initially worked alongside local Chinese banks, especially the *qianzhuang* or 'money shops', which had well-developed local connections and were already highly commercial entities (Cheng, 2003). Western banks provided additional capital to the *qianzhuang* through so-called 'chop loans', or *caipiao*. This was done on the understanding that the *qianzhuang* would lend money to local Chinese merchants specifically for the purposes of buying goods from foreign firms (Nishimura, 2005). The demand for credit and transfer facilities, and, specifically, for institutions which could handle foreign exchange, accelerated rapidly during this period, soon outstripping the capacity of local banks. As such, foreign banks, especially British banks such as the Hong Kong and Shanghai Banking Corporation (HSBC), entered the market as independent entities and quickly began to dominate the local banking sector (Cheng, 2003; Rawski, 1989). Banks from the other so-called 'Great Powers' (Germany, Japan, France and Russia) soon began to compete with the British for banking business in China. The combined international networks and capital strength of foreign banks saw them take control not just of financing foreign trade in China but also, eventually, of issuing banknotes (Cheng, 2003; Rawski, 1989).

The grip of foreign banks on China's financial system was tightened further, however, when the Qing government became obliged to seek foreign loans to pay off a series of crippling war reparations. China's defeat in the first Sino-Japanese war in 1894 and the subsequent *Treaty of Maguan* saw the imposition on China of a war indemnity of 230 million taels (over 7 million kilograms of silver) (Cheng, 2003). An even more burdensome debt was imposed on the Chinese following their defeat in the Boxer Uprising of 1900. The claim made by the eight-nation alliance,[1] in the Boxer Protocol of 1901, demanded payment of 450,000,000 taels (nearly 14 million kilograms of silver), a sum which could only be paid if China became even further indebted to the foreign banks (Preston, 2000). While the foreign banks were quite prepared to advance these vast sums, they demanded the instigation of special taxes to guarantee the loans. Moreover, to add further to the humiliation experienced by the Chinese as a result of their military defeats, the banks demanded that they themselves become the direct collectors of these taxes. Thus, Chinese customs duties, salt tax and railway receipts came to be processed by foreign banks (Cheng, 2003; Peng, 2007). In the 60 years from the first Opium War in 1840 through to the Boxer Uprising in 1900, China was not only overwhelmed by foreign powers in military conflict but also lost control of economic security as well as its nascent banking sector.

In the face of numerous internal and external crises, political and economic reformers in China initiated a 'self-strengthening movement' (1861–1895) aimed at revitalizing the Chinese 'spirit' in the face of foreign domination (Spence, 1990). The movement argued that China should make an effort to 'learn foreign methods' as a means of resisting the foreign powers that were extracting such punishing territorial, economic and political concessions. The key slogan of the movement was 'Chinese learning as essence – Western learning as function' (*zhongxueweiti xixueweiyong*), which was initially aimed at 'learning' about Western military technology (Wang, 2007), as well as Western economics (Warner, 2017).

Later reformers realized that in order to compete with the West, China also needed to know about Western administrative and bureaucratic techniques, economic and educational systems, as well as management methods. In terms of the banking system, we can see a number of changes emerge as a consequence of this. For example, the Imperial Bank of China (IBC), established in 1897 in Shanghai, is regarded as the first modern Chinese bank (*yinhang*) in that, unlike earlier local banks, it was a joint-stock firm where shareholders assumed limited liability. Sheng Xuanhuai (a high-profile government minister and key advocate of the 'self-strengthening movement') noted that 'All business methods pursued by the Imperial Bank of China will entirely follow the regulations of the Hong Kong and Shanghai Banking Corporation' (Cheng, 2003, p. 25). The importance placed on foreign expertise was further evidenced through the appointment of Antony Maitland, a senior manager at HSBC, as the IBC's first general manager (Cheng, 2003). Moreover, the Qing government's sponsorship of Chinese studentships to universities in the US and Europe meant that, at a surface level at least, there was evidence of early convergence in Chinese management practices towards those found in the West (Peng, 2007; Warner & Goodall, 2010). Despite these early efforts by Chinese officials to reform the local banking sector, foreign institutions remained dominant. As well as enjoying the lucrative business associated with collecting the funds to pay off China's foreign debts and war indemnities, foreign banks became heavily involved in handling the personal deposits of Chinese politicians and warlords (Fairbank, Feuerwerker & Twitchett, 1986). Because of their extraterritorial privileges, these banks were able to shield depositors from the scrutiny of the Chinese authorities. During the collapse of the Qing dynasty in 1911, a number of wealthy Chinese bureaucrats and merchants transferred their funds to foreign banks specifically because of their capacity to protect Chinese personal wealth off-shore (Cheng, 2003).

In 1912, however, with the establishment of the Republic of China under Sun Yat-Sen, the fortunes of foreign banks began to change (Spence, 1990). The Republican administration inspired a new wave of Chinese nationalism and a more determined effort was made to challenge the dominance of foreign banks. Twenty-four new Chinese banks were established in 1912 alone, a staggering number when compared with the fact that only 17 had been established in the previous 16 years (Cheng, 2003). Yet it was not until 1929, when the Nationalist government of the *Kuomintang* (KMT) revoked the right of foreign banks to collect the revenue from China's customs and salt tax, that foreign banks' grip on financial power finally began to weaken (Spence, 1990; Peng, 2007). While the influence of foreign institutions diminished, Western methods of financial management and organization were still seen as superior to those found in the local banks (Cheng, 2003; Ji, 2003). Many of the senior managers in the newly established Chinese banks had been educated at Western institutions and, subsequently, sought to introduce Western business methods to local Chinese banks (Cheng, 2003; Warner, 1992). However, the modernization of Chinese banking was curtailed by the events leading up to the Japanese invasion in 1937 (Spence, 1990). Immediately prior to this event, the Chinese Nationalist government, now under the conservative leadership of Chiang Kai-Shek, seized control of 70% of bank assets (Coble, 1986). Following the Japanese invasion, a number of major banks in Beijing were coerced into providing capital to the puppet state of Manchukuo which had been established by the Japanese (Cheng, 2003; Li, 2010). China's domestic banks remained in a precarious position throughout this period, and, following the expulsion of the Japanese in 1945, and the defeat of the Nationalist government of Chiang Kai-Shek by the CCP in 1949, the banks were nationalized completely (Lu, 2007).

The exclusion of foreign banks and the establishment of the monobank: 1949–1978

The dramatic and radical shift in political power that occurred in the late 1940s meant that almost all the foreign banks suffered severe losses. The only Western banks to maintain a presence in the mainland were the two British banks, HSBC and Standard Chartered Bank (Lu, 2007; Peng, 2007). The hostilities between China and the USA (and their respective allies) meant that China's dollar assets were frozen and a series of trade embargos ensured that most foreign transactions, the majority of which were between China and the Soviet Bloc, had to be conducted through barter or reciprocal contracts (Spence, 1990). Throughout the 1950s, one of the principal financial links between China and the rest of the world was a solitary branch of the People's Bank of China (PBC) in Hong Kong. Interestingly, in order for this branch to continue to function properly, PBC relied heavily on the assistance of HSBC. For example, most Sino-Japanese trade, technically blocked by the Americans, was, in fact, conducted through the branches of HSBC and PBC in Hong Kong (Lu, 2007). Furthermore, PBC directed a limited amount of business to HSBC's office in Shanghai during this period. While HSBC described the branch as merely a 'care and maintenance' office, prohibited from financing itself through taking deposits and inter-bank loans, the branch proved useful to the PBC which wished to encourage HSBC to finance Chinese trade by using its own foreign exchange (Lu, 2007). As we shall see, this historically supportive relationship between PBC and HSBC is particularly important for understanding the role of British banks in Chinese financial reform policy in the 1980s and beyond, when 'old friends' were given preferential treatment (Schenk, 2001; Peng, 2007).

In terms of China's internal banking system, the transition to communism in 1949 saw the PBC function both as a central bank and a commercial bank (Naughton, 2007). Its primary function was to allocate financial resources to the SOEs on the basis of strategic policy plans set by central government, the so-called 'credit plans' and 'cash plans' (Lu, 2007). Loans were assigned to the SOEs as described in the government's plans and, consequently, PBC's function as a monitor of the *actual* creditworthiness of SOEs was negligible. The primary objective of SOEs was not to make a profit but to provide stable employment and social services (including housing and hospitals) to their employees (P. H. Nolan, 2001). PBC had no authority to withhold loans, nor any means of pursuing bad debt (Naughton, 2007). In effect, its purpose was to allocate cash resources, and if the borrower (the SOE) refused to pay, the consequences would be dealt with by the government, not the bank (Bowles & White, 1993). This created a situation where the majority of SOEs operated in an environment where there were minimal sanctions for poor financial performance (Lu, 2007; Naughton, 2007). This, along with numerous other political and economic difficulties within China itself, led to a situation where SOEs simply did not repay their government loans. The question of how to address these so-called 'non-performing loans' (NPLs) was ultimately rolled over into the post-1978 period of economic reform (Naughton, 2007). The debts of the SOEs had emerged amidst an intense ideological argument about the very purpose of modern industries: should they prioritize social and communal well-being over the sole pursuit of profit? To untangle their financial difficulties would be no straightforward matter.

Post-1978: reform without losers?

The turbulence created by China's economic policies throughout the 1950s, 1960s and 1970s were the outcome of complex internal power struggles among China's ruling elites. The Great Leap Forward, the Anti-rightist Movement and the Cultural Revolution are just a few of the more quotable examples of policies which had extensive, and, most would argue, deeply damaging, social and economic consequences (Bachman, 2006; Yang, 1996). Each event was the outcome of bitter internal political arguments over the definition and purpose of communism and capitalism in China, the relationship between collectivism and productivity, and China's future position in the world (Vogel, 2011).

By the late 1970s, however, Deng Xiaoping's ideas on the need for a 'socialist market economy', a controversial mix of central socialist planning and market forces, were in the ascendancy (Yang, 1997). A new 'opening up' to the international economy was announced during the 11th party central committee in December 1978 and Deng's aspiration to reintegrate China into the global economy, economically and financially, is evident in policy documents which stated the need for 'active interaction in international financial markets, utilizing foreign capital from various resources, [and] encouraging

FDI [foreign direct investment] inflow, primarily through equity joint ventures' (Lu, 2007, p. 73). At the time, there was a global surplus in investment funds and China, with its virtually un-borrowed status, was, once again, seen as a prime target for foreign banks (Naughton, 2007). However, given the historically difficult relationship between many foreign banks and various Chinese governments throughout the 19th and 20th centuries, the authorities were still deeply distrustful of most foreign financial institutions and, consequently, the activities of foreign banks were severely restricted (Cousin, 2011; Lu, 2007). Throughout most of the 1980s and early 1990s, foreign bank involvement in the mainland consisted primarily of the establishment of representative offices aimed at providing support to the new foreign companies that had entered China to engage in FDI activity, a limited amount of branch development (there were still less than 20 foreign bank branches in China during 2000), and some RMB business (but only with other foreign institutions, and only in a limited number of east-coast cities) (Cousin, 2011; Lu, 2007). The foreign banks that were actually allowed any access at all to the market at this stage were selected because they had, historically speaking, managed to maintain close investment and trade relationships with China (such as HSBC and Standard Chartered), and also because of a perception that their global status could help improve China's standing in international markets (Lu, 2007). Of the 80 or so foreign banks that attempted to establish representative offices in 1980, only seven were granted permission to do so. HSBC, in particular, was given preferential treatment and gained permission to establish representative offices in Beijing, Guangzhou and Shenzhen, and, in 1985, became the first foreign bank to receive a bank licence (Lu, 2007). As noted earlier, HSBC's assistance to the Chinese administration throughout the 1950s and 1960s was not forgotten and proved to be important in re-establishing their presence in the mainland in the post-1978 period.

While HSBC did well in the initial opening-up period (relative to other foreign banks), there were still numerous restrictions on all foreign bank activity at this time. Clearly, the primary reason for this was the fragility of the Chinese banking system itself. Although the initial restructuring of the banking sector had included breaking up the monobank and introducing institutional diversity into the banking system, chronic overstaffing meant that the majority of staff employed in the Chinese banks had low skills and little business awareness, having been trained in an environment where the pursuit of profit had not been the key rationale of the organization (Cousin, 2007). Moreover, each bank was still, at an informal level, obliged to provide credit to local officials for pet projects. Many Chinese banks were, therefore, continuing to support firms on the basis of policy objectives rather than commercial criteria (Cousin, 2011; Naughton, 2007). This period (1978–1993), dubbed 'reform without losers', saw many so-called 'zombie firms' sustained through bank credit rather than through any inherent improvement in organizational efficiency and performance (Lau, Qian & Roland, 2000). On the one hand, it could be argued that this policy was the necessary cost of providing social and economic stability during a period of broader economic transition. Ultimately, however, the practice was viewed as no longer sustainable, and by the late 1990s a large stock of NPLs had developed, estimated to have been in the region of 3.5 trillion RMB, almost a third of China's GDP at the time (Rawski, 1995; Naughton, 2007; P. H. Nolan, 1995). The precariousness of this situation, and the weakness of China's banking system generally, was magnified in 1997 when the Asian Financial Crisis (AFC) sent further shock waves throughout the region. This sharpened the focus of policy-makers on the need to push through ever more rigorous banking and financial reforms (Lardy, 1995).

The precise nature of the political and economic forces that caused the AFC is hotly debated (Corsetti, Pesenti & Roubini, 1999; Wade, 1998). However, most would agree that the liberalization of controls on capital movements in the 1990s, an idea driven by neo-liberal economists and policy-makers based in international organizations such as the IMF, had a significant role to play (Chwieroth, 2007). On the face of it, China appeared to escape any serious effects from the AFC because of its strict control on capital flows and the limited convertibility of the RMB. However, one significant event, which had major consequences on subsequent policy-making in relation to Chinese banking, actually related to the fate of a non-bank financial firm, Guangdong International Trust and Investment Corporation (GITIC) (Cousin, 2011). During the 1980s and 1990s, China's government agencies and provincial authorities had established some non-bank financial institutions which were engaged in various investment activities, the so-called 'international trust and investment corporations' (ITICs). As the mainland banking sector was still largely closed to foreign investors, ITICs were seen as an alternative conduit to China's 'miracle economy' (P. H. Nolan, 2004). GITIC itself was, therefore, particularly appealing to foreign investors who had been wooed by the powerful China 'growth story'. However, far from being the 'financial powerhouse' it was portrayed to be in the international financial media, GITIC had been involved in speculative and high-risk lending during a property boom in Guangdong (P. H. Nolan, 2004).

As a consequence of the regional spillover effects of the AFC, it became apparent that GITIC was engaged in large-scale borrowing which had 'Ponzi'-style characteristics (Cousin, 2007; P. H. Nolan, 2004). The subsequent collapse of the 'property bubble' in Guangdong (another consequence of the AFC) led to widespread insolvencies in the region. However, the biggest shock to the international investment community was that the central government in Beijing actually allowed GITIC to go bankrupt. The assumption of foreign investors up to that point was that GITIC was 'too big to fail' and that their loans were a form of 'sovereign debt', implicitly guaranteed by a communist state that would always save its own companies (P. H. Nolan, 2004). When GITIC filed for bankruptcy in 1999, it owed 46.7 billion RMB (US$5.6 billion), 80% of which was due to international creditors (Xu, 2005). Much to the chagrin of these investors, the Chinese bankruptcy court recognized only about $2.4 billion of their claims against the company and, as of 2003, foreign investors had received only about $300 million, or 12.5% of the $2.4 billion owned (Xu, 2005). The decision to allow GITIC to go bankrupt in this manner led to urgent appeals for the enactment of a new bankruptcy law which provided greater protection for investors (Cousin, 2007; Xu, 2005). From the perspective of the Chinese authorities, however, the move had been essential in order to stop GITIC's problems spreading throughout the rest of the financial system via other domestic trust and investment corporations. What the problem really highlighted, however, was the urgency of ensuring that proper governance mechanisms were established in *all* of China's financial institutions, including its main banks and, crucially, that the ongoing NPL problem be given urgent attention (Cousin, 2007).

The stock problem, the flow problem and the re-entry of foreign banks

While the financial losses incurred during the GITIC incident were largely carried by foreign investors, the event proved deeply troubling to Chinese policy-makers (P. H. Nolan, 2004). A renewed sense of the precarious state of the Chinese financial system led, once again, to efforts to try to move SOEs away from the 'cash vault' model that had dominated the early reform period and led to the production of enormous NPLs (Naughton, 2007). One way of understanding the processes that created the NPLs is to examine the issue from two perspectives: the 'stock' problem and the 'flow' problem. The stock problem 'reflects the legacy of past costs' while the flow problem refers 'to the need to prevent new lending decisions from creating new non-performing loans' (Naughton, 2007, p. 461). As far as the stock problem was concerned, a number of radical steps were taken to reduce the size of NPLs in Chinese banks. First, in 1998, 270 billion RMB in special bonds were issued to improve the capital adequacy ratio of the 'big four' SOBs. Second, in 1999, four state-run asset management companies (AMCs) were established to purchase the NPLs from each of the SOBs. Shifting the bad loans to the AMCs meant, in principle at least, that a 'firewall' was created which separated the bad loans accumulated by the policy-driven lending of the past from the new, supposedly market-driven, loan-making environment of the future (Naughton, 2007). Finally, the Chinese authorities injected an additional US $45 billion into CCB and BOC prior to their listing on the stock exchange in Hong Kong in 2004. A condition of this cash injection was that each bank made significant improvements to their management practices and credit controls (Podpiera, 2006). All in all, considerable improvements were made in the capital adequacy of the big banks, and hopes were high that they would develop any future business on a much surer footing. In other words, it was assumed that resolving the 'stock' problem would ensure future lending decisions would not lead to new 'flow problems' (Naughton, 2007).

However, the 'flow' problem proved in practice to be much more difficult to resolve. A number of commentators had argued that the numerous recapitalizations extended to the SOBs had sent an implicit message to bank managers that they were *still* not strictly responsible for the consequences of their decision-making. This is the now all too familiar problem of 'moral hazard', a feature also found in Western banks following the government bailouts issued to them following the 2008 banking crisis (Cousin, 2011; Naughton, 2007). The supervision of lending decisions made at the branch level remained weak, and loans continued to be extended on the basis of personal relationships (*guanxi* loans), rather than through an assessment of the credit worthiness of the individual or organization applying for a loan (Cousin, 2011). On top of all this, the salaries of both loan officers in branches and senior managers at the executive level were very low, and fraud at both the local and national level was extremely widespread (Cousin, 2011). P. H. Nolan (2004) reports that one of the most serious financial scandals at the time (and there are plenty to choose from) related to the embezzlement of around US$500 million by five bank officials at the Kaiping branch of BOC in Guangdong. Three of the bank's senior officials – Zhu Xiaohua, Li Fuxiang and Wang Xuebing – had effectively found a way of transferring vast sums of the bank's foreign currency reserves to shell companies in Hong Kong. This money was then forwarded on to investment accounts in Canada and the USA. Zhu Xiaohua was sentenced in 2001 for accepting a bribe of 4 million RMB and Li Fuxiang committed suicide by jumping from the seventh-floor window of a hospital. Two of their colleagues, Xu Chaofan and Xu Guojun, received 20-plus-year jail sentences in the US in 2009 for their involvement in the fraud, which included laundering some of the cash through casinos in Macao and Las Vegas (Li, 2009). Because the men were also part of Premier Zhu Rongji's team of financial advisors, their crimes, rightly or wrongly, tarnished his reputation as an 'anti-corruption' reformer (P. H. Nolan, 2004). Consequently, the incident created leadership problems at the highest level of China's political elite. Against this political backdrop, renewed arguments were made that part of the solution to China's banking problems would be to allow foreign banks to fully re-enter the market (Cousin, 2011; Naughton, 2007). Although opening up the sector was part of the mandate for China's WTO accession, the perception among some Chinese policy-makers was that this move had many clear advantages over maintaining the status quo because: (i) foreign banks could increase competition; (ii) they could assist local banks with the introduction of new technologies and financial products; and (iii) they could enhance the corporate governance of local banks, both directly (through joint ventures and shareholdings in Chinese banks) and indirectly (through creating competitive pressures) (Cousin, 2007).

The CCB was the first of the 'big four' SOBs to sell stakes to foreign investors and, in 2004, their IPO in Hong Kong was valued at a staggering US$67 billion (for 20% of their stock). The Bank of America bought 8.7% of the stock and had the option of raising its stake to 19.9% at a later date (Cousin, 2007). Moreover, Bank of America promised to be an active partner, providing technical assistance to the newly listed bank. In return, they gained a seat on the Board of Directors, on the assumption that they would have some say over the future direction of the bank (Naughton, 2007). Other notable examples of foreign investment during this period were Citibank's investment in Shanghai Pudong Development Bank and HSBC's purchase of a stake in Bank of Communications (see Table 3.3 in Chapter 3). Much of the promotional material of the banks at this time portrayed these partnerships as the ultimate 'win-win' scenario. For example, John Bond, Chairman of HSBC, commented on their investment in the Bank of Communications in 2004 as follows: 'For HSBC, this investment provides the group with a new window for developing our business in China. In return, we offer the Bank of Communications the opportunity to draw on our international expertise and network' (LaMoshi, 2004). Similarly, the Bank of Communication's Chairman, Jiang Chaoliang, noted that he indeed hoped very much to draw on HSBC's knowledge and proficiencies so as to ensure 'a quick IPO' (LaMoshi, 2004). In reality, however, despite numerous publicity events aimed at promoting the mutual benefits of foreign bank investments, joint ventures and other kinds of co-operative agreements, the implications of the re-entry of foreign banks to the Chinese market were deeply contested, both internally and externally.

Critics of foreign ownership

Given the decidedly chequered history of foreign banking in China, some Chinese policy-makers remained sceptical about the inherent 'trustworthiness' of foreign strategic investors. Those on the 'new left' of the political spectrum, claimed that foreign banks would simply overwhelm China's financial system and exploit it to their own advantage, as they had done in the past (Freeman & Yuan, 2011). This view was reinforced by a number of incidents which raised serious doubts about the level of commitment of Western investors, despite their superficial claims to understand the importance of 'long-termism' as a core cultural value in China. For example, Ning and Huawei (2005) reported problems relating to the strategic co-operation agreement between BOC and Royal Bank of Scotland (RBS). They noted that two of BOC's directors (who also represented the Ministry of Finance) voted against the deal at the last minute because they felt that RBS was simply not committed enough to bring in the reforms and new technologies that BOC needed. The problem arose when RBS announced that it only intended to purchase a 5% stake in the bank, rather than the 10% initially negotiated (Ning & Huawei, 2005). As well as worries over the commitment of foreign investors, another cause for political concern was that Chinese banks were being sold too cheaply to foreigners, who then gained substantial windfalls following the banks' IPOs. In 2006, a spokesman for CBRC, Luo Ping, said that there was regulatory anxiety about 'selling banks on the cheap' and that the Commission were worried over the 'sincerity' of foreign banks' long-term commitments because 'Foreign investors' penchant for short-term gains undermines long-term business investment and the country's growth potential' (Ho, 2006). Such remarks were indeed prescient in that, in the light of the global banking crisis which began in late 2007, many foreign investors did indeed sell off their investments at the first sign of trouble. The reputational damage caused to foreign banks by this move is discussed in more detail in Chapter 7.

Power and politics in the multiple histories of Western banks in China

In this chapter, we have demonstrated that the history of China's banking sector has been one of struggle, both internally and externally, for domination over political and economic ideas as well as financial resources. Put another way, a number of multiple histories need to be considered, each of which is based on a set of normative assumptions about what matters in tracking the development of the banking sector. For example, the types of resources, or 'capital', which have been valued and pursued range from access to the vast local branch networks of the Chinese banks themselves, through to the sophisticated knowledge of financial products required by China from the West in order to develop a fully functioning capitalist society (credit cards, mortgages and so on). Moreover, some of the changes described in this chapter were the consequence of major exogenous shocks, such as war and revolution; others, however, were the result of more gradual shifts and development. To take one simple example, the commercial successes of the foreign banks in China during the late Qing period led Chinese officials to modernize their banking system through modelling and copying the business practices of foreign institutions. The Qing government required Chinese banking institutions to adopt Western methods, as witnessed through the development of the Imperial Bank of China in the 1890s. These institutions were explicitly modelled on Western ownership models and management methodologies. During the post-1978 reform period, the Chinese authorities once again sought out technical assistance and financial investment from foreigners with a view to modernizing the procedures and products of domestic banks. In their efforts to control the 'flow' problem, which had created such enormous NPLs, they also actively pursued partnerships with foreign banks with the explicit aim of once again modelling the financial expertise and management methods of these institutions.

In some ways, then, these more gradual changes may be described as examples of isomorphic processes in play (Scott, 2008). However, the concept of isomorphism can only be taken so far. As noted in Chapter 2, its emphasis on the role of conformity and 'copying', as a response to environmental uncertainties, overlooks the more complex political and ideological factors contributing to institutional and organizational change. At the most 'overt' level, conflicting political ideologies over the form and function of Chinese society and economy saw huge shifts in the organizational structure of banks. This can be observed in the shift from an independent commercial banking sector in the 1930s to a centrally controlled monobank in the 1950s and

1960s, and through again to the emergence of quasi-commercial, but still state-dominated, banks in the post-1978 era. Power bases were deeply fractured in each of these periods, not just between foreign and Chinese institutions but also within Chinese institutions themselves. Furthermore, the rationalist view of inevitable economic convergence in the banking sector towards models found in the West (discussed in Chapter 2), fails to acknowledge that parts of the business community in China are still permeated by a deep-seated resentment of historical foreign domination. In the build-up to China's WTO accession in 2001, the image of foreigners as 'wolves' ready to rip into China's economy was much in evidence in the popular press (Gao, 2007) – for example, the prominent Chinese economist, Li Yining, observed that 'this time the wolves really are coming' (Peng, 2007, p. 20).

A number of commentators have noted that the political elite in China continues to use historical memory to remind the populace of the humiliations that China suffered at the hands of the Western powers and Japan throughout the 19th and early 20th century (Bickers, 2017; Naughton, 2006; Wang, 2014). Some interpret this 'education campaign' as part of a legitimacy-seeking agenda by the current administration of the CCP (Wang, 2014). By seeking to diminish the class-liberation discourse of the Maoist era, with its potential to focus popular opinion on to the stark inequalities in contemporary China, the CCP directs attention, instead, to the dangers posed by hostile outsiders, in the hope that this may inspire a new sense of national coherence and unity (Callahan, 2012; Wang, 2014). In this sense we see how power operates at a latent level, working to define the political agenda in such a way as to influence the ideas of less powerful groups (Lukes, 1974). More specifically, the events highlighted here also demonstrate how, historically, power has circulated around the banking system, through Chinese policymakers and elites, through the executives at SOBs and, on occasion, through the Western banks and their managers (Clegg, 1989). In order to understand the practices and strategies of the key actors operating in China's banking sector today, it is necessary to understand the socially and historically constructed nature of the organizational field in which they operate. As we will show in following empirical chapters, part of that construction is based on referencing a particular narrative of history which 'never forgets' China's exploitation and humiliation at the hands of outsiders (Wang, 2014, p. 4).

Moreover, as Callahan (2012) notes, the trend in commentary since around 2002 has been the development of a narrative that emphasizes the importance of Chinese 'civilization and culture' in influencing a specific, path-dependent development trajectory (Hamilton, 2006; Redding & Witt, 2007; Warner, 2014a, 2014b). This thread, while originally rooted in empirical studies of Chinese organizations and businesses, has recently gained further traction in popular media, and it is possible, as Callahan (2012) argues, to identify a discourse of 'sino-speak' which 'presents an essentialized Chinese civilization that is culturally determined to rule Asia, if not the world' (p. 33). Callahan reviews and critiques a number of influential commentaries which are gaining traction with policy-makers and the public alike, such as Martin Jacques' *When China Rules the World* (2009) and Liu Mingfu's *The China Dream* (2010) both of which draw heavily on the 'civilizational' narrative. Callahan compares these to more guarded and measured analyses which use Chinese history in a more nuanced way (Horner, 2009; Reid & Zheng, 2009) to draw out the multiple 'truths' which can be found in China's past. He concludes that 'there is no singular Chinese world order, Asian model, or East Asian system' (Callahan, 2012, p. 46).

Callahan's analysis draws attention to some common thematic dimensions in contemporary discussion of China's future such as convergence/divergence, tradition/modernity and East/West, which, he argues, can all too readily lead the reader into an oversimplified view of China's place and future in the world. Jacques (2009), for example, argues that China's 'ancient civilization' makes convergence with 'Western' political values impossible. Callahan notes that Jacques is highly selective in his use of both Chinese and Western history, 'looting' the historical record in a partisan way for events which support the 'China's rise, Western fall' narrative, a story line which is often promoted by the PRC itself. For Jacques, 'there is one China, one Chinese identity, and one proper way to understand China' (Callahan, 2012, p. 36). For Callahan (2012), this narrative of a 'singular' China serves to construct a 'strict East/West geo-cultural framework that is reminiscent of Orientalist projects of the past, except in reverse' (p. 36). Using Roland Barthes (1972) text *Mythologies*, Callahan (2012) points out that what is important is that we understand the emergence of these interpretations of China's past not so much as attempts to identify 'the Truth' about China, but, rather, to acknowledge the way such texts act as 'interpretive logics that [describe] situations, problems and solutions in particular ways' (p. 44). We will in turn see how this characterization applies to later chapters.

Conclusion

This chapter began by discussing one of the most notorious episodes in the relationship between China and the West, namely the 'opening up' to foreign trade forced upon China following the Opium Wars (1840–42 and 1856–60). This period, and the associated decline and eventual fall of the Qing dynasty in 1911, saw Western banking institutions dominate China. During the turbulent decades leading up to World War II, the Republican and Nationalist governments began a concerted effort to modernize Chinese banks and to resist the continuing expansion of foreign banks. Following China's own civil war, and the establishment of the communist government in 1949, the influence of foreign commercial banks evaporated and the state monopoly banking system was established. The reforms initiated in 1978 by Deng Xiaoping saw the economy shift back from central planning towards a more market-based system. The reasons for allowing Western banks to re-enter the market at this stage were based on the belief that free market competition, a reduction in the extent of state ownership and revised government regulations would increase the organizational efficiencies of Chinese banks, making managers more accountable for their decisions. In other words, many of the macro-level policy decisions were based on the core assumptions underlying rational choice economics, a remarkable ideological turnaround in such a short period of time. However, the move was not without its critics and there has been a growing resistance to the reforms from those on the 'new left' of China's political spectrum. This serves to illustrate that Chinese politics is most certainly not unified and homogenous, and diverse and conflicting factions continue to influence policies in many ways. At a more theoretical level, the significance of these events for understanding institutional change and power relations in the field of banking has been outlined. Based on a selective review of the historical record, foreign investors may be presented as threatening and untrustworthy and, consequently, can find themselves restricted in their business activities. However, it is also important to understand that the construction of the past in contemporary China rests on a specific political narrative promoted by the CCP. By emphasizing the historical wrongs that China has suffered at the hands of outsiders, the extent of internal injustices and inequalities may be downplayed (Wang, 2014). Many of the themes identified in this chapter will be echoed in later chapters both through the interviews with participants and in the analysis of policy documents issued by Chinese and Western opinion-makers. Following Callahan's analysis, this material reveals 'multiple truths' about organizational practices in China's banking sector.

Note

1 Austria-Hungary, France, Germany, Italy, Japan, Russia, United Kingdom and United States of America.

5 Regulating the banking sector

conflict and control in enforcement regimes

The regulation of banking activity in China, as elsewhere, is influenced by informal societal values as well as formal laws (Kwak, 2013; Redding, 2005). In China, these values influence economic rationales in such a way that the objectives of organizations include an emphasis on maintaining social stability and re-establishing China's place in the global order, as well as improving profitability. In this chapter, we will investigate the different, and sometimes conflicting, rationales that have been adopted in China as officials attempt to build a regulatory framework for the banking sector. The question we seek to answer here is: How does state-level policy influence the meaning attached to new banking regulations by different actors, interest groups and organizations? It is certainly possible to identify a government *narrative* which emphasizes the importance of adopting regulatory models based on international 'best practice' aimed at improving standards in domestic banks. Yet it is also the case that certain regulations are structured, interpreted and enforced in ways that disadvantage Western banks.

Despite a surface-level appearance of convergence towards international norms, we will show that a national style of regulation – and more particularly enforcement – is in play, which limits the activities of foreign banks. In other words, the nature of the regulatory field in China reflects a political process driven by informal objectives aimed at protecting domestic banks from being overwhelmed by foreign competition. As with other key strategic industries, such as energy and telecommunications, the Chinese administration is promoting home-grown 'national champions' who will dominate the domestic market in banking and financial services (P. H. Nolan, 2014).

In this chapter, we demonstrate how Western bankers and their representative organizations attempt to resist these practices by drawing on orthodox economic arguments that it is only through 'open' market competition and 'light touch' regulation that China can improve domestic banking efficiency. Unsurprisingly, this argument has not gained traction with many Chinese policy-makers, particularly following the events which led up to the financial crisis of 2008. We will provide evidence which indicates that, from the regulator's point of view, the *partial* enforcement of regulations has, in fact, provided a supportive environment for the domestic banks. Sufficient (if not optimum) levels of organizational efficiency have been achieved. In an environment where a nationalist discourse aimed at reasserting China's position in the global arena is of paramount importance, there is little to be gained from allowing Western banks full market access and 'fair' treatment.

The development of banking regulation in China

This section focuses specifically on how China's membership of the WTO, and associated involvement with the Basel Accords,[1] shaped the development of the key regulatory institution in China, the China Banking Regulatory Commission (CBRC). China achieved WTO accession in 2001; however, given the historical difficulties faced by the banking system, a transition period of a further five years was granted, with full opening-up occurring in December 2006. One of the key requirements of membership of the WTO is that the applicant nation open its economy to international competition (Cousin, 2011); consequently, a new set of bank licensing requirements were established, ostensibly to ensure parity between foreign and domestic banks. Key changes included relaxing the requirement that foreign banks choose a Chinese bank as a joint-venture partner. Foreign banks were also allowed to target Chinese customers as well as foreign investors, and RMB trading was opened up more widely. Finally, constraints on geographical location were eased and foreign banks could establish operations outside of the east-coast cities (Cousin, 2011).

As discussed in Chapter 2, for many academic commentators influenced by rational choice economics (see, for example, Sachs & Woo, 2003), China's pursuit of WTO membership was an indication that policy-makers viewed the convergence of Chinese financial institutions with those of advanced market economies as both necessary and desirable. Opening the domestic banking sector to foreign competition, a key requirement of WTO membership, was seen, in principle, as a way of sharpening the organizational efficiency and competitive edge of local banks. However, before foreign banks could be given wider access to the market, it was necessary to establish a regulatory body with clearly defined supervisory powers. Consequently, the CBRC was established in 2003 as part of the modernizing agenda associated with WTO membership (Naughton, 2007). The establishment of the CBRC saw the regulatory function of PBOC separated off from the ownership and daily management of the banks (as noted in Chapter 3, the PBOC had previously acted as both regulator and shareholder creating potential conflicts of interest). Indeed, the range of responsibilities given to CBRC indicated that bank supervision appeared to be moving away from political and administrative control towards a system based on legal authority, technical expertise and market-based principles (Cousin, 2007). The regulatory independence of the CBRC was clearly stated both in the *Law of the PBOC* (2003) and the *Law on Banking Supervision and Administration* (2006). The laws aimed to ensure that there was fair competition between institutions, with a view to raising their efficiency and effectiveness. CBRC was also charged with licensing banking institutions, conducting off-site and on-site supervision and inspection, approving the capacities and qualifications of senior managers, as well as resolving banking crises or high-risk situations (Cousin, 2007). CBRC's documented responsibilities now include ensuring banking institutions keep to the law and that they maintain the trust of the public. Taken together, these responsibilities indicate that, in principle at least, regulation is based on norms which value the role of competition in improving performance, consider professional management training important and take seriously the implementation and enforcement of the rule of law.

In order to gain credibility, the CBRC has drawn on numerous international frameworks to develop its own regulatory system (Cousin, 2011). These include supervision based on the CAMELS system and adopting the Basel Accords (García-Herrero, Gavilá & Santabárbara, 2006; Yan & Huang, 2008). The CAMELS acronym reflects six key assessment areas, namely: capital adequacy, asset quality, management, earnings, liquidity ratios and sensitivity to market risk (Hafer, 2005). The CAMELS rating system was originally developed in the late 1970s as a means for assessing the market risk of US banks, but was adopted by many other nations over the following decades (Bauer et al., 1998). The rating system provides a score which indicates to the national regulator the particular market risk of a specific bank. In 2004, CBRC used this system for a systematic peer group comparison of the domestic banks (García-Herrero et al., 2006). Then, in 2005, they introduced legislation which allowed the regulator to enforce changes in banks, including changes to senior management, supervisory take over, and bank closure (Loechel, Packham & Li, 2010).

Similarly, the Basel Accords were considered important tools for driving through domestic reform. The argument was made that, as 'external' mechanisms, they could be used as 'impartial' tools to impose discipline on a field divided by factional local elites and other powerful vested interests (Shih, 2008). A Council of International Advisors (CIA) was also appointed to offer advice on how the sector could best adapt to the various Basel Accords (Loechel et al., 2010). At one level, the establishment of the CIA could be interpreted as an attempt to demonstrate that China was, in fact, actively seeking convergence on regulatory mechanisms that had perceived international credibility. This was especially important during the early 2000s, the period leading up to the IPOs of the Big Four state banks. The CBRC described council members as having:

> assumed high positions in the international financial institutions [and having been involved in] formulating international banking standards or in the financial supervisory bodies of the developed economies. They have profound theoretical attainments and ample practical experiences in financial supervision and enjoy high international reputation.
>
> (CBRC, 2003a, para 2)

The membership of the 2003 committee is shown in Table 5.1, along with a list of more recent appointments.

The appointment of members of the CIA illustrates how CBRC is attempting to gain international credibility for their procedures. The formation of the council is a public act which indicates that the regulator views the expertise of overseas authorities as an important source of validation for its own reform processes (Fligstein & McAdam, 2012).

In brief, regulatory reforms aimed at opening the sector to international competition were presented to the outside world as an essential element of the reform process. Reflecting on the strategic investment made by HSBC in the Bank of Communications in 2005, the then Finance Minister, Jin Renqing, argued that, given the enormous size of China's foreign currency reserves, it was not particularly interested in HSBC's 19% capital investment in the Bank of Communications. Rather what was needed was their 'management and technology, because the authorities do not want to have to recapitalise this

Table 5.1 Members of the Council of International Advisors

Council members appointed in 2003
Mr Andrew Sheng,* Chairman of the Hong Kong Securities and Futures Commission
Mr Andrew Crockett, Former General Manager of the Bank for International Settlements
Mr Edward George, Governor of the Bank of England (at the time of appointment to the committee in 2003)
Mr Howard Davies,* former Chairman of the Financial Services Authority
Mr Gerald Corrigan,* former President of the Federal Reserve Bank of New York
Mr David Carse, former Deputy Chief Executive of the Hong Kong Monetary Authority
* Members marked with an asterisk are still on the Council as of September 2015
Council members appointed since 2003
Ms Sheila Bair, Former Chair of Federal Deposit Insurance Corporation
Mr John Bond, former Chairman and director of HSBC Group
Ms Laura Cha, former Deputy Chair of Hong Kong's Securities and Futures Commission and Chair of Hong Kong's Financial Services Development Council
Mr Roger Ferguson, President and CEO of TIAA-CREF; former vice-chair of the Board of Governors of the Federal Reserve System
Mr Stuart Gulliver, group CEO of HSBC Holdings plc, Chairman of HSBC
Mr Ian McFarlane, former Governor of the Reserve Bank of Australia and non-executive director of ANZ
Mr Tom de Swann, former CFO of ABN Ambro and former Chair of the Basel Committee
Mr Jean-Claude Trichet, former governor of the Bank of France, former President of the European Central Bank

Source: CBRC, 2003b, 2016.

bank every other year' (Cousin, 2007, p. 54). At the time there was a public discourse that convergence on Western banking practices was the best way forward for Chinese banks (Cousin, 2007). Given the rather abysmal performance of Chinese banks in previous decades (see Chapter 4), there was a belief that the incorporation of more market-orientated systems, which welcomed foreign competition, would improve the efficiency, credibility and reliability of domestic banks (Naughton, 2007).

Yet despite these public commitments to formal regulation, market competition and international convergence, the CBRC needs to be understood as an institution which ultimately lacks political independence. As is the case with the Chinese banks themselves, CBRC is staffed with senior members of the Communist Party, selected specifically by the State Council, and regulators are still required to seek the approval of the State Council for most major decisions (Brehm, 2008). As such, CBRC is not an independent regulatory entity and its policy direction remains heavily influenced by the State Council (Cousin, 2011). Although there is evidence, at a macro level, for convergence on international banking norms, there are also numerous examples of formal regulations which undermine foreign banks, as well as many inconsistencies in the actual enforcement of regulations which clearly work to the advantage of domestic banks. Assuming that banking reforms are based simply on a normative, international 'best practices' approach fails to acknowledge the inherent embeddedness of the regulatory framework in a political process which actively seeks to prioritize Chinese interests first (Brehm, 2008; Pearson, 2005, 2007).

Economic nationalism in the regulatory field

Implementation of the WTO protocols

In this section, we will demonstrate that China's WTO accession protocol did not create the much anticipated 'level playing field' for foreign banks. To do so, we will draw on official documents issued by the European Union Chamber of Commerce in China (EUCCC), the American Chamber of Commerce in China (ACCC), and interview data collected over the course of our investigations (see Methodological Appendix for further details). In a number of annual surveys, the EUCCC has reported that many of its members had doubts about China's willingness to implement WTO commitments (EUCCC, 2009, 2010a, 2010b, 2010c). In 2010, for example, the EUCCC Annual Business Confidence Survey demonstrated that only 21% of respondents felt that China was implementing changes in the spirt of the WTO agreement. Moreover, 26% felt that China was actively seeking loopholes to avoid or delay implementation (EUCCC, 2010b). The EUCCC also reported that although China has signed the WTO's government procurement agreement, delays in implementation were interpreted by members as wilful 'stalling'. The report concluded that members increasingly perceived that failures to enforce WTO obligations were 'deliberate attempts to circumvent trade rules rather than owning to a lack of resources' (EUCCC, 2010b, p. 20). The most significant obstacle for professional services firms was reported as the 'discretionary enforcement of broadly drafted laws and regulations' (EUCCC, 2010b, p. 27).

The ACCC also reported that its members were dissatisfied with China's implementation of the WTO accession process. They noted particularly that members were concerned that the policy objective of creating 'national champions' had led to 'government interference in markets to determine which companies should succeed' and that this 'would reduce the space for open cooperation and competition between US firms and their foreign counterparts, reducing quality, competition and depriving the Chinese market of important foreign expertise' (ACCC, 2009a, p. 18). Moreover, the ACCC argued that this policy was 'counter to the principles of national treatment and non-discrimination' laid out in the WTO protocol and as such was likely to 'hinder' competition and 'harm' companies (ACCC, 2009a, p. 18). From ACCC's perspective, such behaviour was counter to China's own interests. They asserted that:

> There is a clear tension between promoting open, competitive markets and encouraging domination by domestic companies. ... This short-term goal of promoting domestic industry comes at the cost of competitive pricing, world-class technology and long-term market efficiencies, and may arouse retaliatory policies abroad.
>
> (ACCC, 2009a, p. 20)

The ACCC also argues that to ensure effective implementation of new laws, there needs to be greater capacity building at the provincial and local levels. They express concerns that poor enforcement creates opportunities for abuse which:

> improperly favour local firms or those in good stead with local officials. This reduces efficiency, fosters corruption and hampers short and long-term development ... Inconsistent and opaque implementation and enforcement of important measures persist at all levels of government, particularly locally.
>
> (ACCC, 2009b, p. 16)

Similarly, the EUCCC noted that 'the spectre of protectionism has also appeared and European companies are increasingly concerned by the tendency for local companies to be favoured over foreign-invested ones' (EUCCC, 2010b, p. 6).

In brief, the regulatory environment in China was perceived by foreign businesses as possessing a distinct bias towards domestic firms. Both the ACCC and the EUCCC were concerned that regulatory favouritism towards domestic firms prevented 'good' business decisions and discouraged foreign investment. Interestingly, both institutions argued that this situation was detrimental not just to foreign organizations but to Chinese institutions as well. Both worked from the unquestioned assumption that open market competition inevitably improves organizational efficiencies, regardless of political, historical or cultural context.

Banking regulations

Further problems (from the point of view of Western banks) can be found when we turn specifically to examine the development and implementation of banking regulations from 2006 onwards. The EUCCC reported a number of significant difficulties. First, they noted that members reported a lack of coordination between different Chinese authorities which led to inconsistencies in the implementation of licence requirements for new financial products and services (EUCCC, 2008). Western interviewees in this study also noted that they felt that officials themselves were uncertain not just about the rules, but also about where newly evolving power bases might be forming (n=31). Recalling his experience of attempting to get a license for internet banking, one chief representative officer noted:

> I think one problem is that you don't really know who sits on the power. There are different layers, different ministries, different persons, and they themselves have not decided who has got the power. So, we don't have a clear picture of who is in charge, and, I think, neither do they.
>
> (Interviewee #8)

The ACCC noted similar concerns that:

> approvals [for licences and new products] are often required from numerous regulatory agencies that have different approaches to the approval process and different interpretations of the rules and regulations.
>
> (PricewaterhouseCoopers, 2008, p. 79)

These examples illustrate the somewhat unpredictable nature of power within the 'circuit' of regulation (Clegg, 1989). While Western banks may be sensitive to inconsistencies in the application of regulations, organizational outcomes are not always predictable or readily 'explained' by reference to the 'overt' face of power (see Chapter 2). Power and influence are moving rapidly within the regulatory field and it is difficult for Chinese administrators to keep up with the changes. However, there are other examples that demonstrate more clearly the overt face of power in the regulatory sector, specifically as it relates to disadvantaging the Western banks. A clear illustration of these problems can be found in the development of the *Bank Card Policy* in 2007. This policy stated that foreign banks must:

> build *within* China data processing systems which can meet the technical standards required by the business and possess the technology to protect information security.
>
> (EUCCC, 2010c, p. 436, emphasis added)

In brief, the policy required that before they could be granted a licence, foreign banks were required to relocate their data-processing systems (in relation to Chinese business customers) to the mainland (EUCCC, 2010c). Previous regulation had only required that the data-processing systems were 'safe and efficient' and did not stipulate a precise geographic location (EUCCC, 2010c). Members of the EUCCC argued that this change in policy was particularly problematic for them because the majority of foreign banks were global in scale and already had data-processing centres in place in East Asia, if not China itself. They noted that:

> Setting up a specific China platform would represent considerable extra costs for international banks ... by requiring banks to set up their onshore processing capacity before the business has started and making it a condition for the business licence approval puts foreign bank at a competitive disadvantage compared to domestic banks.
>
> (EUCCC, 2010c, p. 437)

A number of participants felt that the real reason behind this policy was that the Chinese authorities were attempting to use their facilities to create a reliable credit databank on the Chinese mainland which could then be 'seized' and accessed by domestic firms at a later date (n=16). Individual credit rating systems are in a nascent form on the mainland and the opportunity to access such data in the future will be much easier if the processing systems are physically located on the mainland rather than offshore. As one IT director noted:

> The Chinese are unsure how to do this [develop an individual credit rating system], and really, they don't think their own banks will do it properly. So because they like our systems they'll get us to do the donkey work and then just take the data. And they can only do that if the systems are physical based here, not in Singapore or wherever.
>
> (Interviewee #27)

As well as problems with bank card regulation and data processing, the ACCC (2009b) also expressed concerns about the nature of regulations controlling forms of ownership. Specifically, they noted that (i) locally incorporated foreign banks were, in practice, still not allowed to acquire local banks, and (ii) non-locally incorporated banks were not allowed to acquire more than 20% of domestic banks. ACCC argued again that these restrictions on ownership act as a form of protectionism and discriminate against foreign banks. Again they revert to the argument that this practice is also damaging to the domestic banking sector because:

> The goals of improved management, technology and risk management are not fully realised by limiting foreign banks from obtaining higher stakes in local banks.
>
> (ACCC 2009b, p. 188)

As well as problems with formal regulations, our participants also report numerous examples of difficulties caused by *informal* discriminatory practices. An example of this relates to the tussle over developing credit card facilities. In 2014, the WTO ruled that China had 'illegally' favoured China UnionPay (China's only domestic bank card) over international competitors such as Mastercard and Visa (Lu, 2012). Although Mastercard and Visa have been accepted in China for quite some time, it was not until 2015 that they were allowed to seek licences to clear domestic Chinese payments (Wildau, 2015). Prior to this, Chinese citizens could only use credit cards issued by China UnionPay, which has a limited network abroad. China UnionPay, a direct competitor to Mastercard and Visa, is principally operated by the larger state owned-banks (ICBC, ABC, CCB, BOC) and the PBOC ('China UnionPay', 2016). In turn, PBOC has the authority to decide whether foreign banks can put Mastercard and Visa facilities on the cards they issue in China. Clearly, this can create conflicts of interest and situations can emerge where policy objectives aimed at providing support to domestic banks may override WTO regulations aimed at ensuring open competition. Participants interviewed for this study noted that China's bank card policies limited their ability to compete with local banks (n=22). One informant reported that his bank was facing real difficulties because it had been refused a bank card licence by PBOC, ostensibly on issues related to the design of the card. The original design of the card had included both the Mastercard and UnionPay logo but had been rejected:

> They said they don't like the design of the card. But then they approved the one with only the UnionPay logo on it. Why didn't they approve the one with both logos on it? It's protection. It's to keep the Mastercard and Visa out. And the key thing is that they want UnionPay to gain more acceptance outside China. If they get us foreign banks using it – and their systems - within China then it'll be easier to pressure us to use it outside China in a few years' time.
>
> (Interviewee #35)

Even in 2013, after the WTO ruling, the PBOC blocked a partnership between Mastercard and a domestic online payment platform which prevented Mastercard from issuing RMB-settled credit cards (Wildau, 2014).

Other examples included difficulties in obtaining retail banking licences. One regional CEO described how shortly after the opening of a new branch on the mainland, he was informed that the rules had changed and the location of the branch, on the first floor of a shopping centre, was no longer allowed. He was required to close it and move it to the ground level where no empty units were currently available. He interpreted this as a deliberate attempt to sabotage his business:

> They do it on purpose. They do it deliberately to screw you over. And in one sense I don't blame them, every country protects its own banks first, but they won't stop me – I'll still find a way to make money here.
>
> (Interviewee #6)

By focusing attention not just on formal regulations but also on informal regulatory practices such as these, it is clear that the regulatory environment is a field where there is a power struggle between many different groups, each pursing different and conflicting objectives. While central government officials may have developed some regulations in line with their WTO commitments, there is a perceived lack of consistency in implementation which obstructs the development of Western banks. Power struggles and other forms of resistance in the host society tend to be overlooked in models of institutional change which are driven by the assumed universal benefits of open market competition. In order to make sense of this situation, the influence of local and state-level power bases, networks and spheres of influence must also be taken into consideration (Redding, 2005; Whitley, 1992). In sum, evidence from both documentary analysis and from key informants indicates that senior decision-makers in Western banks were frustrated by unclear regulations, inconsistent regulatory implementation, and lack of transparency. Some of this may be explained by the 'lack of capacity' and disorganization among officials at the provincial and local levels, but much was interpreted as a deliberate strategy aimed at restricting the development of foreign competition in the banking sector. However, it should not surprise us that, where possible, policy-makers and enforcers seek to disadvantage foreign banks. Given the widespread historical narrative (described in Chapter 4) that emphasizes China's past exploitation at the hands of the West, it is to be expected that levels of mistrust are high.

Post-crisis banking regulation

The credibility and trustworthiness of Western financial and economic values received a further blow following the 2008 financial crisis. More specifically, failure in the assumptions underpinning banking regulations is now seen as one of the key antecedents of the crisis. Indeed, in the 2009 G-20 Summit, the *Leaders' Statement* claimed failure in financial regulation was the 'fundamental' cause of the crisis (G-20 Communique, 2009). Catastrophic failures occurred because the attitudes underpinning regulations assumed that 'light touch' supervision was best and that unrestricted market forces would lead to the efficient allocation of capital (Coffee, 2009). As a consequence, the meeting of the G-20 in 2010 passed the new Basel III accord which called for tighter regulations and higher capital adequacy requirements. In China, the regulators became increasingly vocal in citing their views on the importance of strong state regulation in the banking sector. They began to articulate their opinions not just about regulations but also about the role of Western economic values in causing the crisis. This is best illustrated by reference to interviews given by Liu Mingkang, Chairman of the CBRC from 2003 to 2011. In an interview with the respected Chinese financial journal, *Caijing*, Liu noted that developing robust banking regulation in Western countries was 'only in words, not in deed'. He argued that 'laissez-faire in regulating was a mistake', and that 'in the financial world, market failures occur often, and relying on the self-regulation of financial institutions is far from enough to protect the system (Li, 2009, para 16). Liu also criticized the conduct of the board members of failed Western banks, noting their 'lack of responsible behaviour' and he critiqued the 'myopic' nature of the US bailout which 'shifted from saving banks to saving auto companies', a move he considered 'damaging and confusing' (Li, 2009, para 20). Finally, he disagreed strongly with the view that financial innovation should not be regulated, a key argument used by the Wall Street elite to influence US regulations, noting that 'the top duty for a bank regulator is to protect depositors and other financial product customers' (Li, 2009, para 22).

Similar themes are found in his article for the *Financial Times*: 'Basic Rules' (Liu, 2009), where he advocated a return to 'old-fashioned rules' in global bank regulation. He argued:

> In an increasingly interconnected world, financial risks now spread like pandemics. One of the effective ways to prevent risk contagion is to set up firewalls between banking and capital markets … Unfortunately, many people have forgotten this principle, or dispute it as 'old-fashioned'.
>
> (Liu, 2009, para 4)

Further support for his views on the value of a 'simple' mode of banking regulation can be found in his comments that:

> We insist that the main funding source of banks should always come from deposits. On top of that, the CBRC is developing a regulation that would require firewalls to be established between commercial banks and their controlling shareholders and between commercial banks and their non-banking subsidiaries, in order to prevent risk contagion … Practice shows us that traditional tools work, especially considering that financial engineering can malfunction.
>
> (Liu, 2009, para 8)

Chinese banks were, of course, relatively unaffected by the financial crisis. The main reason for this was their very partial exposure to sub-prime assets and their limited integration into international financial markets (Loechel et al., 2010). Indeed, the rapid decline in the market capitalization of some Western banks saw the Chinese institutions ascend towards the top of the global bank ranking in 2009 (see Table 3.1). However, in many ways, Chinese banks were simply lucky with their timing. Liu Mingkang's post-hoc analysis of events, which focuses solely on the prudence of CBRC's 'sound' regulatory approach, does not give us the full picture. Prior to the 2008 crisis, Chinese banks were, in fact, very interested in developing 'risky' products. For example, Man (2009) reports that some of the Chinese banks who had strategic partnerships with Western banks (such as the now divested partnerships between Goldman Sachs and ICBC and between China Construction Bank and Bank of America) had been using their foreign connections to sell overseas derivatives to domestic clients. There are also several examples of Chinese companies 'taking a haircut' on these more exotic financial products. *Caijing* cites the case of Citic Pacific which lost HK$15 billion on foreign exchange hedging, and China Eastern Airlines Corp which booked a 6.2 billion RMB fair value loss on wrong-way bets on fuel hedging contracts (Huiyin, 2008; Zhou, 2009). After the event, *Global Times* (a Chinese newspaper published by the *People's Daily*, the official newspaper of the CCP) reported that the CBRC had brought in new regulation to curb these practices, noting that: 'The CBRC firmly opposes the trading of high-leverage, complicated and opaque derivatives, as well as those irrelevant to the needs of the real economy' ('CBRC Moves to Regulate', 2009). In the same article, one CBRC official described derivatives as 'financial opium', a metaphor no doubt chosen to remind his audience of the exploitation China suffered at the hands of the West during the Opium Wars and hinting at the need for China to guard against Western abuse and manipulation in the contemporary banking sector.

In sum, it is possible to identify a regulatory philosophy in China which, while encouraging 'efficiency through market competition' at a surface level, still regards the protection and promotion of domestic banks as its key objective. It is fair to say that a suspicion of the potentially destabilizing influence of foreign financial institutions has impacted on the current implementation of laws. It should not surprise us that Western banks complain about the development of regulations which disadvantage them or of the unreliable ways in which regulations are enforced. It is not in China's interests to make life easy for them. As one of our participants, a regional CEO, noted:

> We must understand the Chinese regulatory system and we, being a foreign bank, must adapt our system to this Chinese reality. And we can see this as a protectionist system to support their own banks. Or we can see it as a cautious system. CBRC is looking at all these new instruments and saying they don't want those problems. So those smart bankers in New York, who thought it would be a good idea to give every unemployed guy in Alabama a loan to buy a house, come along here and say they have

> ideas about how to develop this market, of course the Chinese won't be taken in by that!
>
> (Interviewee #33)

Organized interests and the development of banking regulations in China

An important part of the comparative business system approach, as introduced in Chapter 3, is to examine the way in which organized interests (be they the state or firms) try to reproduce positions of power and control. In this chapter, we have focused particularly on the way in which Western bankers, and their representative bodies, interact with China's regulatory institutions. In doing so we have outlined the contradictory conceptions of control that influence that relationship. In the Western context, states create regulatory agencies which, technically speaking, generate rules that impartially control the interactions between firms, workers and states (Fligstein, 2002). However, regulatory agencies in the West, especially those in the UK and the USA, have often been heavily influenced by large global multinational corporations (MNCs) and dominant domestic firms. This form of 'regulatory capture' occurs through political lobbying and other forms of personal influence such as job promotion (Baker, 2010). An oft-quoted example of an institution prone to regulatory capture in the West is the Securities and Exchange Commission, the regulatory body of financial services in the USA (Kwak, 2013). This institution has long been criticized for its tardy approach to investigating fraud and insider trading on Wall Street and for its tendency to rely heavily on advice received from the very individuals it is supposed to regulate (Kwak, 2013). In brief, we need to understand banking regulation as an outcome of cultural, historical and political contexts, whether that is in the US, China or any other part of the world. International convergence in regulatory practice may be observable at the level of formal policy, but we should expect to find differences in implementation and enforcement in different national contexts.

For example, Loechel et al. (2010) compared the mission statements of regulators in France, Germany, the UK, the US and China and found that they shared the key aims of ensuring market confidence and stability, protecting deposits and customers, and maintaining high standards of market conduct. Although the regulatory goals of each country were broadly similar, in China they noted that there was a more overt emphasis on the role of banks in promoting economic growth. They argued that policy in China: 'reflects the clear preference of Chinese regulators for *stability* instead of *efficiency* as the primary goal' (Loechel et al., 2010, p. 20). Certainly, the CBRC has made clear its intentions to guide banks to support macro-economic policies and regional development policies (CBRC, 2006). As it stands, Chinese regulators have been tasked with maintaining the stability of the system while simultaneously attempting to develop the domestic sector through allowing limited exposure to foreign competition. Consequently, ideas about the deregulation and liberalization of banking regulation which dominated thinking in the pre-crisis West are unlikely to gain a foothold in China for foreseeable future. Indeed, Western bankers, accustomed to having great influence over policy-makers in their home countries, find themselves with little power and influence over Chinese regulators. The enduring control of the Chinese state over the banking sector, driven by a desire to prioritize financial and economic security over organizational 'efficiencies', ensures that their ideological influence is limited. This is not to say that Chinese regulators do not believe that greater competition could drive further improvements in domestic banks. However, the extent to which that competition will come from *Western* banks is sure to be limited. These institutions have provided useful operating models for domestic banks, but it is unlikely that they will be given opportunities to develop to their full capacity in mainland China. Ultimately, we could conclude that the 'informal' aim of regulatory policy in China is to see domestic banks dominate the field and compete among themselves.

Conclusion

The first part of this chapter illustrated how CBRC aimed to reform domestic banks through adopting an international 'best practice' approach to regulation. This was achieved through involvement with organizations such as the WTO and a commitment to the Basel Accords. The appointment of foreign advisors to the CIA was also an important step towards gaining credibility for the reform process. The second part of the chapter showed the restrictions which were, in practice, placed on foreign banks and limited their ability to compete in the Chinese market. We emphasized that such practices are not confined to China. The way in which banking regulations developed in the West has long been influenced by perceptions of what best suits the interests of politically connected elites. In China, the regulatory structures tend to favour domestic banks and this can include the composition of formal regulations as well as the 'arbitrary' enforcement of existing regulations. Organizations such as the ACCC and the EUCCC may emphasize the 'dangers' of protectionist and discriminatory practices in regulation, insisting that they will inevitably encourage inefficiencies in domestic banks too. However, what the Western 'efficiency' arguments miss are the roles of substantive rationality and historical memory in influencing the development of the banking market in China. It should not surprise us that, where possible, policy-makers and enforcers seek to disadvantage foreign banks. China's regulators are not convinced that fully opening their nascent banking sector to foreign competition is appropriate, despite attempts by Western bankers to persuade them otherwise. While increasing the profitability of domestic banks is an important goal, the underlying rationale of regulation is to ensure China's continuing economic development and to restore China to a leading position in global economic order. In other words, the case of banking regulation demonstrates that there is more than one way to organize a sector 'efficiently' and in China this does not include making life easy for Western banks.

Note

1 The Basel Accords refer to recommendations on banking regulations issued by the Basel Committee on Banking Supervision (BCBS). Basel I (published 1988) was concerned primarily with credit risk; Basel II (published 2004) sought to establish international standards on capital adequacy; Basel III (published 2010) was designed in response to the 2008 financial crisis and made further recommendations on levels of capital adequacy, stress testing and market liquidity risk. The Basel Committee is composed of representatives from central banks and the regulatory authorities of all G-20 economies and other major banking centres. The committee cannot enforce recommendations although most member countries will implement their policies. (See Basel Committee (2010) for further details.)

6 Western investors and corporate governance reforms in Chinese banks

In this chapter we examine the nature of corporate governance reform *within* Chinese banks. Our principal question is to discover whether joint-ventures and foreign investment improved the corporate governance of Chinese banks and what kind of corporate governance model is emerging in the sector. First, we provide an overview of the development of corporate governance in China, highlighting the influence of Anglo-Saxon economic thought on early reforms. Then we move on to analyze interviews with those of our participants who were involved in strategic partnerships between Western and Chinese banks. We focus on themes such as the perceived effectiveness of Western non-executive directors, the practice of senior Chinese managers holding political appointments and the lived experiences of managers involved in technical assistance projects aimed at improving corporate governance (see Methodological Appendix for further details). We will once again draw attention to the way in which political context and cultural preferences can influence business rationales. In China, the state uses its controlling stake in large banks for goals other than increasing shareholder value and this necessarily places foreign minority shareholders at a disadvantage.

Defining corporate governance

Academic definitions of corporate governance vary according to the political standpoint of any given researcher. Orthodox definitions, based on rational-choice economics, focus on forms of corporate ownership, the structure of the Board of Directors, and the implications of these factors for *profit maximization*. Here, the concern is with examining the role of corporate governance in alleviating the so-called 'principal–agent' problem – that is, the difficulties which can arise in trying to ensure that agents (in this case managers) do not act primarily in their own interests, but in the interests of another party (namely stockholders, or 'the principal') (Jensen & Meckling, 1976; Shleifer & Vishny, 1997). Another set of related conflicts can occur when majority shareholders pressure managers to act in ways which benefit their interests, often to the detriment of minority shareholders (Porta et al., 1998). In this chapter we will see worked examples of both these issues. Other definitions of corporate governance focus not just on the relationship between managers and shareholders but on a broader range of interest groups. For example, one economist, Margaret Blair, defines corporate governance as 'the whole set of legal, cultural and institutional arrangements that determine what publicly traded corporations can do, who controls them, how that control is exercised, and how the risks and returns from the activities they undertake are allocated' (Blair, 1996, in Clarke, 2011, p. 78). From this perspective, corporate governance includes understanding how power relations, informal social networks, cultural preferences and historically situated institutions impact on corporate governance and related management practices.

Studies of *comparative corporate governance* foreground how problems of governance are dealt with in different national contexts (see Zhang, 2017). In the West, it is possible to distinguish at least two forms of corporate governance. First, the *Anglo-Saxon* model (principally found in the US and the UK) based on prioritizing shareholder interests and a belief that this is best accomplished through lightly regulated, decentralized markets. Much of the work on the principal–agent problem described above emerged from this area of study. Second, the *Continental European* model, which is based on a stakeholder theory of the firm, and examines the interests not just of shareholders, but of other groups, such as trade unions, employee work councils and the societies in which firms operate (Aguilera & Jackson, 2003; Luo, 2007). It is also possible to identify several distinct corporate governance models in East Asia, including the *Keiretsu* model in Japan (sets of companies with interlocking relationships and shareholdings) and the *Chaebol* model in South Korea (composed of government-supported global conglomerates such as Samsung) (see Campbell & Keys, 2002; Witt, 2006). In China, corporate governance practice is evolving but it is possible to identify a *control-based* model in those industries (including banking) where the state remains the controlling shareholder (Liu, 2006, Nolan, 2010). Here the strategy has been to diversify the ownership structure of former SOEs with a view to improving operating performance while simultaneously maintaining administrative control of key industrial sectors. The field of comparative corporate governance often focuses on whether or not there really is one model which is universally more effective than others. We will argue that the market-based model developed in the US and the UK, and often prioritized in policy circles, cannot be expected to operate in China's banking sector without modification. This is not just because of the scale and complexity of the structural and cultural differences between the different regions, but, more fundamentally, because the Chinese administration is pursuing a different set of social policy objectives than is commonly found in the West.

The evolution of corporate governance in China

The 1980s saw widespread international interest in the ideas and methods underlying the corporate governance systems used in Japan and Germany.

However, 'fashions changed' in the early 1990s, when the Anglo-Saxon model gained greater ascendency, due, in part, to the seemingly greater robustness and dynamism of the US economy (Clarke, 2011). It was during this period that corporate governance reform in China began in earnest and policy-makers at the time were influenced by the US model. From 1984 to 1993, a separation of government and enterprise took place. In 1993 an Anti-Unfair Competition Law was introduced, and from 1994 to 2005, a new Company Law bedded down. After 2006, a mixed-ownership model came into being (Zhang, 2017, p. 360). The goal was to restructure the SOEs (which included the monobank) through the introduction of divisible equity shares, and through changes in management structure. The newly formed corporations were now steered by a *Board of Directors* who would be accountable, in principle, to external shareholders. Such steps also made the new corporate arrangements more acceptable vis-à-vis China's membership of the WTO.

Transforming the PBOC from its monobank status into a series of smaller entities would allow non-state actors (including foreign investors) to become involved in the new corporations as more visible and present principals who, in turn, could pressurize and monitor managers directly. The state-owned banks which were established in the early 1990s (see Table 3.2) were now run by a Board of Directors which was staffed with independent directors, including foreign non-executive directors, who supervised the company's senior management. The Board of Directors, in turn, was overseen by a Supervisory Board which was tasked with notifying shareholders of any significant problems. In this sense, there are similarities with the Anglo-Saxon model, in that the main responsibilities rest with the Board of Directors; however, the presence of the Supervisory Board draws on the two-tier structure commonly found in the German model (Cousin, 2011).

As noted earlier, the regulations governing the ownership and management of modern Chinese corporations are described in the Company Law. The law states that the general shareholders' meeting represents the highest authority and, to quote Cousin, 'should make decisions in relation to policy and investment, choose directors, approve reports from both boards, decide on the distribution of profit and loss, the organisation of the company as well as any mergers' (Cousin, 2011, p. 203). From the perspective of the Chinese administration, the view in the late 1990s was that part-foreign ownership could be particularly helpful in improving internal governance structures such as risk management and performance incentives, as well as helping with the development of new technology and products (Cousin, 2011). Indeed, much of the narrative on the inclusion of Western investors in the reform of the banks rested on the view that corporate governance itself was a kind of 'technology' which could be readily adopted through technical assistance projects. Moreover, the inclusion of a well-known foreign brand name was believed to provide greater opportunities for attracting funding for the banks' IPOs, leading to further diversification of ownership (Leigh & Podpiera, 2006). There is certainly some evidence that so-called 'technical assistance' projects between Chinese and Western banks worked reasonably well (Hamid & Tenev, 2008). One of the most quotable examples are the investments made by the International Finance Corporation (IFC) in several city commercial banks, the China Minsheng Banking Corporation and a number of rural credit cooperatives in the early 2000s (IFC, 2012). In addition to their equity investments, the IFC engaged in technical assistance to facilitate the transfer of internal corporate governance practices, credit analysis, risk-management practices and the development of internal lending controls. On the one hand, the IFC emphasized that foreign banks have, in the main, had a positive influence on the development of corporate governance in Chinese banks. However, they also noted that Western corporate governance systems could not be transferred in a straightforward manner. In retrospect, they acknowledge that greater sensitivity could have been exercised in attempting to impose such systems in less developed parts of the country (IFC, 2012). Despite some surface-level similarities with ownership and management structures found in parts of the West, the discourse, laws and cultural institutions underpinning corporate governance in China remain somewhat different to those encountered in other parts of the world (Clarke, 2003; Zhang, 2017). Indeed, much of the separation of powers described in the Company Law is somewhat meaningless, given the interconnected nature of the agents involved. Despite the policy rhetoric around the need for diversified ownership, state ownership remains high in strategically important sectors of the economy, including banking, and while some non-state actors have entered the arena, they remain minority shareholders with little control or influence. Furthermore, while the state is looking for ways to improve the efficiency of its enterprises, profit maximization is not their only objective. Their aims also include maintaining control over sensitive industries, using directorships and other senior management posts as conduits for political job placements, and ensuring some stability in urban employment through controlling the flow of credit to certain 'pet projects', especially in the construction industry. In China, because the state uses its controlling stake in banks for goals other than increasing shareholder value, the foreign minority shareholder is placed at a distinct disadvantage. In a review of international investors' perspectives on the continuing dominance of the state as the key shareholder, the Institute of International Finance (IIF) notes that the Supervisory Board is very often restricted and in practice has little more than a 'rubber stamp' function (IIF, 2006). So, to all intents and purposes, the contemporary ownership structure of China's largest banks has notable similarities to the one that existed prior to the reforms. As we shall demonstrate in the following section, the introduction of a Western-influenced system of corporate governance has been contested both at the level of economic principle and in day-to-day management practices.

The system in practice

Legitimacy-seeking as a rationale for seeking foreign investment

As described above, the basic methods employed for improving corporate governance have included initial public offerings on the international stock markets, strategic partnerships with foreign banks (also with the aim of improving management and product development) and the inclusion of overseas board members on the Board of Directors (Cousin, 2007). In the Chinese context, foreign ownership has been shown to improve the market valuation of a company, mainly through an increase in investor confidence by the association with a well-known international brand name. This situation continues to the present day (see Warner, 2014a). Historically speaking, diversified ownership was thought to be an important tool for improving governance, because of its assumed power in helping to align management and shareholder interests. In the Anglo-Saxon model, shareholders are assumed to be widely dispersed, and when they are dissatisfied with the performance of a company, they may sell their shares. So the share price is assumed to be a sensitive indicator of performance, and if a senior manager underperforms, this will be reflected in a low share price. This, in turn, may lead to their dismissal. In other words, their job security is bound to the performance of the firm. However, the relevance of this approach is highly questionable in the Chinese context for a number of reasons which will be explored in detail below. Many of the Western participants interviewed for this aspect of the research (n=40) were sceptical about the utility of the model in the Chinese context, not least because of the low levels of influence that foreign investors experience in their day-to-day activities. As one director involved in a co-operation agreement pointed out:

> I'm cautious about over-stating the influence of foreign investment in reforming the banks. Our experience hasn't been good. Obviously, we remain minority shareholders and have no rights … the way they see it, is that they are in control and they're going to do what they like. They want us to help them develop their consumer credit cards and that's it, they really have no interest in us as far as corporate governance issues are concerned.
>
> (Interviewee #29)

This example illustrates the difficulties in simply assuming that foreign investment will automatically align managers' and shareholders' interests, as it might do in other more market-orientated regimes. Given that the limits on foreign share-ownership are capped at 20%, state-owned banks, like other large SOEs, are not, in fact, exposed to the market rigours and ownership pressures which advocates of the Anglo-Saxon model believe create robust governance systems. Indeed, numerous participants (n=32) noted that the belief that a foreign investor had any significant influence over governance issues in China was simply naive. Most emphasized that it was the *belief* of those outside the region that foreign investment could help create good governance within the firm that was important. A management consultant who had been involved in the IPO listing of a major Chinese bank argued that:

> When you're looking at a 'big name' deal with one of the State-Owned Commercial Banks, it's done mainly because of the branding. Really the Chinese bank isn't that interested in advice about governance, what they want is to get listed on the Hong Kong market, and for that a foreign brand name really helps. These guys aren't comfortable with strict rules. So everyone just pretends that everyone needs governance advice but actually they [Chinese banks] don't really pay any attention to this.
>
> (Interviewee #15)

This observation highlights the view that legitimacy-seeking has been an important motivating factor among Chinese executives seeking foreign investment, at least in those IPOs that occurred prior to the 2008 financial crisis. (See our discussion of the Agriculture Bank (ABC) of China IPO in 2010 in Chapter 8 for more recent shifts away from this perspective.) To the extent that, historically speaking at least, Chinese officials wished to develop an international profile for their major corporations, including the banks, they needed legitimacy in the eyes of their international business peers. From the perspective of participants in this study, however, practices within the organizational context are lagging behind the publicly stated aims of officials. This can perhaps be most clearly recognized in the perceptions held about the relative ineffectiveness of foreign non-executive directors.

Perceived ineffectiveness of foreign non-executive directors

In the Anglo-Saxon model, internal control mechanisms, such as the structure of the Board of Directors, are thought to be essential for the establishment of sound corporate governance systems because they ensure clarification of lines of responsibility and help prevent conflicts of interest between agents and principals. A small group of participants (n=8) were relatively optimistic about the role foreign board members played in this aspect of corporate governance in Chinese banks. A Western consultant who was closely involved with the IFC reform project observed that:

> it is very clear that the foreign-appointed non-executive director in a Chinese bank makes a contribution of genuine value … and this includes such things as the establishment and monitoring of credit committees and supervisory committees and they absolutely do help to maintain standards of corporate governance that simply would not be otherwise maintained.
>
> (Interviewee #13)

While acknowledging that changes in board composition and the establishment of supporting committees was an evolving 'process', these informants remained optimistic in their assessment of the influence of foreign non-executive directors, pointing out the now almost ubiquitous adoption of separate credit and supervisory committees in Chinese banks and the significance of these institutions in normalizing governance structures. Those who were confident about the role of non-executive foreign directors on boards were, however, in a distinct minority. Most participants questioned about this issue (n=32) were unconvinced about their ability to effect change even if they had contributed to the foundation of new organizational structures. A senior executive at a locally incorporated foreign bank pointed out that:

> They have no influence, the board doesn't feel any real obligation to take on their advice, the overall direction of the Bank is determined by the majority shareholder, i.e. the Communist Party, the appointment of any influential board member is made by them and that person may be technically and managerially quite competent, but ultimately they're motivated by factors which are not commercial and they think about their career in terms of political progression as much as anything.
>
> (Interviewee #20)

As noted by Clarke (2011), while the Company Law may in principle offer protection for minority shareholders, legal institutions, such as courts, law firms and other routes for private litigation are all rather weak and exist on the sufferance of the government. Chinese courts are unlikely to be involved in cases involving powerful private plaintiffs and large sums of money unless they are called upon to do so by the political elite (see, for example, the case of the former mayor of Chongqing, now imprisoned, Bo Xilai). In this sense, majority shareholders are indeed vulnerable and they have few formal institutional supports with which to pursue any grievances (Porta et al., 2002). Furthermore, there are blurred boundaries in managerial roles and responsibilities and many senior executives also hold high-level political positions within the CCP.

Political roles of senior Chinese managers

Principal–agent relationships are complex in China because 'profit maximization' for the principal is not the only motivating factor for managers. Most executives in the large banks see further career advancement in both the political and business spheres, and almost all have previously held high-ranking political appointments. Table 6.1 shows the dual roles held by bank Chairmen as of January 2013. Consequently, the motivation of senior Chinese managers are also driven to a certain extent by party loyalty which can, on occasion, conflict with other, more market-orientated objectives.

Table 6.1 Chairmen of key Chinese banks and previous official positions (as of January 2013)

Bank name	*Chairman's name*	*Previous official positions*
State-owned commercial banks		
ICBC	Jiang Jianqing*	Member of Central Committee of CPC, PBOC
BOC	Xiao Gang	Member of Central Committee of CPC, PBOC
CCB	Wang Hongzhang	Chief Disciplinary Officer of the People's Bank of China
ABC	Jiang Chaoliang	Member of PBOC and SAFE. Deputy Governor of Hubei Province
Joint-stock commercial banks		
BoComm	Hu Huaibang	Director of Supervisory Committee CBRC Commissioner of Discipline Inspection CBRC
Merchants	Fu Yuning**	
SPDB	Ji Xiaohui	Shanghai Municipal Government
Minsheng	Dong Wenbiao	Party Secretary of the CPC Committee, member of the CPPCC, PBOC
Industrial	Gao Jianping*	
Everbright	Tang Shuangning*	CBRC PBOC CCB
Huaxia	Wu Jian*	General Manager and Secretary of Leading Party Group of Beijing Branch of Bank of Communications, Member of Leading Party Group, Head of Discipline Inspection Team

Sources: Cousin, 2011, p. 118; Annual Reports; Company Websites.
* Also mentioned as Party Committee secretaries in the annual reports.
** No previous official positions found but was a member of the Twelfth National Committee of the Chinese People's Political Consultative Conference (CPPCC) in 2013.

On one level, this need not be problematic. In the Chinese context, the dual political and commercial roles that senior managers occupy leads to the addition of an important disciplinary mechanism. Because managers in the state-owned banks are members of the CCP, appointed by the Party Organization Commission, they are subject to investigation by the Central Discipline Inspection Commission (CDIC). This body can in certain circumstances impose severe punishment on managers who are involved in graft (indeed, economic crimes of sufficient magnitude may sometimes carry the death penalty). In 2007, the CDIC announced 'strict prohibitions on the use of state official positions to gain improper benefits' and also directly monitors 'individuals with special relationships' who are defined as those with 'close familial relations, mistress/lover relations, or other relations of common interests with state officials' (Cousin, 2011, p. 287). However, before it can act, the CDIC must, in the first instance, report to the Party

Secretary in an organization. As outlined above, the Party Secretary in the state-owned banks may also be the Chairman of the bank and so the degree of relational interconnectedness between the parties involved may make it difficult for this system to work fairly and impartially in practice (McGregor, 2010; Warner, 2014a).

In brief, the state continues to exercise control both through the monitoring agencies (such as the CBRC), through shareholder voting, and through more traditional routes such as the authority of the CCP to appoint key personnel. Clearly, then, the adoption of a corporate governance system based on the assumptions commonly found in the Anglo-Saxon model, such as diversified ownership, robust legal systems and meritocratic recruitment of senior managers, is not necessarily the most appropriate form for the Chinese business context.

The limits of technical assistance projects

As was shown in the earlier discussion of IFC technical assistance projects, co-operation between foreign and Chinese banks was viewed as an important means of implementing credit-checking systems and risk-management procedures, systems which are particularly important for the establishment of good corporate governance. However, as we shall see below, the view that corporate governance is a simple matter of 'technical assistance' fails to capture the complexities of organizational life that managers encounter in their daily practice. The participants interviewed in this study who were also involved in technical assistance projects (n=26) noted that there are major hurdles in actualizing knowledge transfer of any kind. One executive noted:

> The practicality of it is that we don't have any way to do the technology transfer. We don't have anybody really of consequence to go in and train the people. And the Chinese can't get access to the people that they need to because they are not in Asia, they're in America. And so what do we do, we say, put your hand up everybody who speaks Chinese. We find some relatively low-level people in America, we find some people here and there. … And then you hear great things in the newspaper [about technical assistance]. But then you go and talk to the rank and file and it's like: 'Get me out of here, this is awful, it doesn't work'. They feel they are going into a situation that's completely contrived.
>
> (Interviewee #26)

On one level, such accounts simply alert us to the difficulties of initiating organizational change when skills deficits run high on both sides. However, it was also clear that participants perceived that in the majority of cases 'technical assistance' in corporate governance was no longer a chief requirement of the partnership; the main objective of collaboration was, once again, to boost international investor confidence in the company. A regional CEO observed:

> But your typical guy who is working at a relatively senior level at a bank in China has more exposure to state of the art credit scoring and credit analysis than anybody in a US bank, and then these American guys are sitting there trying to sell it to them. The Chinese know what they're doing now; it has nothing to do with that anymore, they know how to do all that. This is nothing to do with learning from [US Bank] – that's all nonsense. It's a show for everybody outside the region. That's what it's for.
>
> (Interviewee #23)

Indeed, participants believed that it was not a lack of 'know how' that impeded the development of effective credit rating, but, rather, enduring organizational and cultural factors. Given the history of Chinese banks as policy lenders facing few commercial pressures, there has been little need for credit-checking and risk-management procedures. In particular, the distribution of so-called *guanxi* loans is still perceived to be widely practised. These are loans which are issued according to the extent and interconnectedness of the social and business networks of branch managers and borrowers, rather than conventional credit criteria such as borrower assets and repayment history. As a senior manager noted:

> Typically, the problem with the Chinese banks I've worked with is that, well, the provincial governor, his brother is running the bank and the customers are working on building up those links. Then those people in the top positions approve the credits then those people start falling behind and don't pay back. That's the biggest problem in the Chinese banking system today – those *guanxi* credits.
>
> (Interviewee #41)

Indeed, in surveys conducted for the central government, Xie and Lei (2005) reported that 45.5% of respondents stated that it was necessary to 'bring forward some advantage to the bank officer' in order to get a loan (in Cousin, 2011, p. 202). Liu Jiayi, auditor general of the National Audit Office, reported that financial investigations in 2008 revealed that 6 billion Yuan ($878 million) was misused in 20 major cases. About half of the cases involved three of China's biggest state-owned banks: ICBC, BOC and CCB (Zhen, 2009). That the loans were examples of 'serious illegality and economic crime' was largely attributed to the fact that the loans were granted not on the basis of risk-management principles but on a 'who you know' basis, as *guanxi* loans. Implementing a valid and reliable personal credit rating system in China is unlikely, therefore, to be significantly influenced by the introduction of foreign investment and technical assistance projects. A much more fundamental shift in the cultural influence of *guanxi* would be required. Indeed, Western participants noted that the influence of instrumental *guanxi*, based on the material aspect of gift and favour exchange, was a major dilemma in co-operation agreements. Many (n=31) noted occasions when they had been put in a compromising position by Chinese partners attempting to build networks for the business. As regional COO noted:

> A couple of drivers were using our cars to take important people down to the local massage parlour. And it was [the Chinese partner] who told them to do it. And this one night these guys got arrested, but I'm the one who gets a call at 4.00am, and the sergeant of the police said, 'You tell me these are good boys and they can walk'. But I said, 'No', and they got charged. And my lawyer said, 'I'm glad you did that, because otherwise he [the police sergeant] would be on the phone to you tomorrow wanting payback', because all of a sudden, I owe him you know, 'We're friends, we're here to help you out', that kind of thing. Got to be so careful with *guanxi*. If you take it you've got to give it back.
>
> (Interviewee #54)

Western media have made much of the problem of corruption in China, with a particular focus on high-level elites. Of course, corruption is in no way confined to East Asia, and Western business are also embroiled in similar scandals even though the monitoring mechanisms and legal systems in the region are more robust. Indeed, Bracking (2009) notes Western businesses are frequently involved in bribery cases in developing countries, with records indicating that bribes of around £53 billion were paid in 2001 alone (with the arms and construction industries among the worst offenders). What is important for our purposes here, however, is that by focusing on the lived experiences of managers involved in technical assistance projects aimed at improving corporate governance we recognize their inherent 'messiness'. Focusing solely on change at the institutional level overlooks the role of long-standing cultural patterns and politically motivated policy objectives on the path-dependent development of corporate governance.

Implications for the Chinese model of corporate governance

This chapter has investigated the variety of institutional and cultural factors that have influenced the adoption of Anglo-Saxon corporate governance practices in Chinese banks. Internal governance mechanisms, such as the Board of Directors, and diversified ownership structures have been widely adopted. The perception of our informants, however, was that as the state is the majority shareholder in most banks, then the inclusion of foreign shareholders and non-executive directors cannot be a seen as a solution to the principal–agent problem in China. It was the view of participants that the main reason for including foreign directors on the board or of pursuing part-foreign ownership was to enhance the perceived legitimacy of Chinese banks in the international financial community. Similar themes were found in the examination of technical assistance projects related to establishing credit-rating and risk-management practices.

While regulators may still aim for international standardization, at the level of the organization, there is little will, and few incentives, to change current practices. More interestingly, however, the themes presented here raise interesting debates about defining 'problems' in the study of comparative corporate governance. Many of the early reforms were driven by attempts to adapt Western solutions to the 'agency dilemma' to the Chinese context. Separation of ownership and control is crucial to resolving this problem in the Anglo-Saxon model but not so much in other regions, such as China. In other words, to quote Clarke, 'Organisations can be "efficient enough" if other socially and politically valued objectives are to be met' (Clarke, 2011, p. 9). So does it really matter if the agency dilemma in China has yet to be resolved? For whom is the principal–agent problem a 'problem'? To some extent, answering these questions depends on the goals and interests of the particular organization and the society in which it is embedded. If social and political goals are highly market-orientated, with profit maximization seen as the only means of achieving treasured 'efficiency' gains, then it is indeed a problem. If, on the other hand, policy goals are orientated towards 'maintaining social stability' through gradual transition, then there is more flexibility in balancing the interests of organizations with those who use their services or are employed within them. Of course, matters are always somewhat more complex than this simple dichotomy indicates. Both standpoints may also have other, unspoken, outcomes, such as the maintenance of the vested interests of established elites in different societies.

Conclusion

The Anglo-Saxon model assumes that, in order to survive, companies must adopt those forms of ownership that provide the greatest possibility for 'efficient' operation, and in general this is taken to be a form of ownership that does not involve large shareholdings by the state (because of the assumed 'agency' costs). The assumption that convergence on Western, particularly Anglo-Saxon, models of corporate governance was likely to occur in China was, to a large extent, informed by neo-classical economic assumptions that market forces have the power to efficiently allocate credit unaided by state 'interference' (Luo, 2007). However, the listing of the 'Big Four' banks on the international stock markets were deals that ultimately took place under government direction and the relationships with external shareholders were not strongly influenced by market forces. Our findings show that initially 'legitimacy-seeking' was important, but, in later listings, such as with ABC (see Chapter 8), the need and desire for strategic partnerships has been much diminished.

Moreover, practices such as a 'who you know' credit culture and the enduring importance of *guanxi* mean that the influence of foreign banks on corporate governance reforms in China is perceived by informants as usually ineffective. There is no doubt that the assumption that market forces and managerial incentives alone can ensure the most efficient allocation of money throughout society was severely tested following the 2008 financial crisis. In this regard, it is interesting to note that the 'control-based' model of governance, which is common in China, where the state takes a guiding role in ensuring that financial intermediation does not upset social stability, has now been adopted as a policy by the UK and US and, even mid-decade, 'quantitative easing' remained *de rigueur*. Of course, the fact that the Chinese state has access to abundant funds to recapitalize inefficient banks or to replenish large-scale thefts should not detract from the need for more fundamental changes in governance structures. But as the 2008 financial crisis has shown, this is in no way a particularly Chinese 'problem'.

7 Networking strategies of Western bankers

power, opportunism and *guanxi* connections

In this chapter, we seek to investigate the role that Chinese power–money social networks play in the networking strategies of Western bankers at the organizational level. We will critically examine what it is that outsiders mean when they talk about *guanxi*, how they justify certain behaviours in relation to *guanxi* practice, and the consequences of their beliefs and behaviours for institutional change in the banking sector more generally. We will demonstrate that *guanxi* practice is not only driven by culture and tradition but is also bound up in a contested exchange of highly valued resources, including both financial and human capital. Consequently, in the arena of global banking, *guanxi* practice is concerned with power relations. In the following sections, we will first outline current debates in the study of *guanxi*, and then examine how Western bankers attempt to build *guanxi* networks focusing on 'relationship hires' and the problems and prospects with this practice. We will then turn to our interview data to investigate why Western managers think *guanxi* is important, how they experience it in their organizations, and the strategies they use to develop *guanxi* networks.

Current approaches to the study of *guanxi* networks

In a very general sense, the term *guanxi* is often used to indicate the existence of some sort of *social relationship* such as a friendship, classmate or a kin connection (Chen, Chen & Huang, 2013). There is also a separate phenomenon, *guanxi* practice (or *guanxi xue*), which refers to the material aspect of relationship-building in China sometimes described as the 'manufacturing of obligation and indebtedness' (Bian, 2018; Yang, 1994). A very significant element of *guanxi* practice is concerned with building obligations through gift and favour exchange (Yang, 1994; Bian, 2018). In his recent review of the research, Bian (2018) develops a five-level model which identifies different types of *guanxi*. He suggests that *guanxi* influence depends on whether *guanxi* is 'a tie of connectivity, a sentimental tie, a sentiment-derived instrumental tie, an instrumental-particular tie, or an obligational tie that facilitates power-money exchanges' (Bian, 2018, p. 1). In this chapter, which examines Western bankers' efforts to build *guanxi*, we will focus mainly on the latter kind of *guanxi*, that which rests on power–money exchanges.

When examining the influence of *guanxi* on institutional change in China, it is possible to identify two theoretical positions. First, there are a group of researchers who maintain that *guanxi* and *guanxi* practice are distinct from the forms of networking found in other societies and that they are a unique feature of Chinese culture. Much of this research takes as a foundational assumption that China is a particularistic and collectivist society and subsequently seeks to describe *guanxi* and *guanxi* practices in relation to other aspects of social life in China, such as sentiment (*ganqing*), human feelings (*renqing*), face (*mianzi*), and reciprocity (*bao*) (Barbalet, 2017; Chen et al., 2013; Nolan, 2012). Research in this area might tend to focus on *guanxi* in terms of familial connectivity and sentimental ties as described above by Bian (2018). From this perspective, it is *culture* that largely generates the rules which define the framework of institutional order (Redding, 2005). In other words, informal institutions are established through social interactions and networks, are relatively enduring and are less open to change than formal, regulatory institutions. This is what we might call a 'bottom-up' approach to institutional development, where the base level of informal institutions of culture and meaning are the key drivers of larger-scale formal institutions (Redding, 2005). As noted in Chapter 2, some scholars in this tradition tend to favour the view that the significance of *guanxi* practice in the period of economic reform has *increased* as the stresses and strains of the transition to a market economy means that people need to utilize informal connections to ensure their economic survival and prosperity. A number of studies have found that *guanxi* practice increased in the reform period, partly as a means of resisting new lines of official and bureaucratic power (Bian, 2018; Yang, 1994).

The second theoretical perspective argues that as legal and economic institutions change, reliance on *guanxi* practices will decline (Gold et al., 2002; Guthrie, 1998; Wank, 2002). Here the key assumption is that changes in formal institutions will act in a 'top-down' way and, given sufficient time, will drive changes in informal networks as we would expect from the convergence thesis. The key example of this perspective on *guanxi* is the work of Guthrie (1998), who argued that a conscious attempt on the part of the Chinese government to rationalize business practices, coupled with increasing efforts to reduce the influence of informal networks in public life, means that *guanxi* practice is in decline as China develops a 'rational-legal' system based on formal laws and procedures. It is central to his argument that rationalization processes, competitive pressures and the nascent development of the rule of law mean that Chinese firms are now less in need of *guanxi* practice to get things done. Moreover, he argues that those Chinese companies involved in joint ventures with Western investors 'copy' the business practices of foreign investors that they perceive to be successful, through a process of 'mimetic isomorphism' (a concept introduced in Chapter 2).

Yang's (2002) critique of Guthrie's thesis highlights several problems with his study, including a narrow sample, a tendency to accept the claims made by Chinese managers at face value, and a limited focus on what *guanxi* is used for in business circles. She argues that *guanxi* is deeply rooted in Chinese culture, consists of a highly resilient repertoire of behaviours and is therefore likely to adapt to new institutional arrangements. Similarly, Chang (2011) argues that *guanxi* varies according to the degree of institutional uncertainty in any given context. The more uncertain people are about information, resource allocation and market competition, the more likely it is that instrumental *guanxi* will flourish. As Bian (2018) argues, information and the influence of power are especially important for the obligational-tie *guanxi* that facilitate power–money exchanges. The ability of Westerners to form the connections they need with influential Chinese business people and policy-makers is, therefore, influenced by what it is they can offer in the *exchange* process. For Westerners, this kind of relationship necessarily involves the exchange of *favours*. In this regard, Western executives may act opportunistically and attempt to adapt to the local environment, rather than alter it, and so the base-level cultural frameworks remain relatively unaltered.

The 'problem' of institutional change

The assumption in the late 1990s by Chinese policy-makers was that the introduction of foreign banks, and their managers, would bring about desired change in the banking system because competition would increase efficiency, and, at a micro level, new actors would unsettle dominant practices and impose preferred alternatives (Cousin, 2011; Mahoney & Thelen, 2010). In other words, as Guthrie and others had assumed, mimetic isomorphism would occur as Chinese banks would replace their systems and management practices with those used in foreign banks, which they perceived to be more successful. This position assumes that meritocratic management practices would develop rapidly and that the most 'efficient' banks would survive and flourish because, among other things, they would contain the most competent and talented individuals.

However, as we have seen in earlier chapters, there is much ambiguity in rule interpretation and enforcement in China's banking system and a great deal of discretion is exercised in how any particular organization develops its business. In such circumstances, individuals who attempt to capture resources and redeploy the prevailing rules to suit their own ends are likely to flourish. Mahoney and Thelen (2010, p. 29) describe these individuals as 'opportunists' who 'do not need to pursue insurrectionary strategies since gaps between rules and enactment are available for them to exploit'. Because they make no effort to actively change existing rules, their behaviour partly explains why changing institutions is more difficult than defending them. In China's banking sector, ambiguities in the interpretation and implementation of existing rules provide the space for opportunists to redeploy these rules in ways that suit their own interests. With these concepts in mind, we will now investigate some of the networking strategies that have been adopted by Western bankers in China, drawing out the consequences of their actions for institutional change. We will first examine the practice of 'relationship hires' in Western investment banks, drawing on high-profile cases reported in the financial press. Next, we will investigate how our participants described and used *guanxi* in their own networking practices, demonstrating the enduring influence of instrumental *guanxi* in China's banking sector.

Relationship hires in Western investment banks

Large Western investment banks are particularly interested in building political connections in China, just as they are in other parts of the world (Paulson, 2015). One way in which they are alleged to do this is through so-called 'relationship hires' where they recruit the relatives of senior officials (often referred to as 'princelings' or '*taizidang*'). The rationale underlying this practice is that the personal and professional contacts of the 'princeling' may help create new business opportunities and confer other advantages on the bank, such as easing the passage of the bank through complex bureaucratic and regulatory processes. In some cases, the appointment, particularly at a junior level, can also be a way of simply demonstrating 'good will' towards the hire's powerful relative, with little expectation that the individual themselves needs to perform at a high level. This could be seen as an example of instrumental *guanxi* in operation, where Western executives seek to create an exchange network in the hope that the favour will be returned at a later date. The financial media has made much of this practice and many allegations have appeared in print. For example, in 2010, John Garnaut, the China correspondent for the Australian publication, *Sydney Morning Herald* and *The Age*, reported that several foreign banks had hired relatives or close associates of Politburo member Wang Qishan who pioneered Chinese investment banking in the 1990s (Garnaut, 2010). Similarly, the well-respected financial magazine *Euromoney* ran an article in 2007 identifying UBS's appointment of George Li, son of a former Politburo member Li Ruihuan, and Merrill Lynch's appointment of Janice Hu (now at Credit Suisse), the granddaughter of former party leader Hu Yaobang (1915–1989) (Wright, 2007).

In some ways, there are valid reasons for hiring such well-connected individuals. In countries, such as China, where codes of practice and regulations are in development, the administrative bureaucracy can be unpredictable and difficult to navigate. A person who has grown up in a family that has influence in this system is likely to have a good understanding of how it works in practice. In this sense, political knowledge is a legitimate form of expertise which is of value to a Western bank. However, difficulties arise when Western banks attempt to adapt to what they perceive to be local cultural norms, especially when they are incompatible with home-country anti-corruption rules. Examples of Western bankers who have fallen foul of this dilemma include Garth Peterson, an American vice-president at Morgan Stanley's property investment office in Shanghai. Peterson was fired in December 2009 on the suspicion that he had a violated the US Foreign Corrupt Practices Act (FCPA), a law which aims to eliminate the practice of paying bribes to overseas public officials. He was eventually sentenced to nine months in prison for the offence (Dye, 2012). Peterson, a fluent Mandarin speaker, had developed a strong *guanxi* network among local officials in Shanghai and had allegedly appointed relatives within Morgan Stanley (Chen & Eder, 2009). More recently, JP Morgan was fined $264 million by US authorities to settle charges that they had breached anti-bribery laws by employing 'princelings' to secure business worth more than $100 million (Martin, 2016). The Security and Exchange Commission (SEC), the US regulatory body, said staff at JP Morgan in Asia circumvented the organization's recruitment practices by setting up the 'Sons and Daughters' scheme in 2006 which actively encouraged government officials to put forward relatives for jobs. The misconduct was described as 'blatant' by the SEC, with bankers keeping records of the business that came from customers who had acquired jobs for their children in this way. At the time of writing, HSBC and Citigroup Inc. are also under investigation by the SEC for recruiting employees based on their relationships (Yu, 2017). HSBC issued a statement noting that the investigation related to recruitment practices based on referrals by 'government officials or employees of state-owned enterprises in Asia-Pacific'. They also noted that they could not predict 'the resolution of these lawsuits, including the timing or any possible impact on HSBC, which could be significant', (Cassin, 2016).

In brief, the opaque nature of China's political and economic framework, coupled with the enduring influence of high-level *guanxi* connections, places foreign banks in a dilemma. It may not be straightforward for bankers to demarcate between the need to be sensitive to local cultural norms, the expectations that they deliver a profit to their organization, and the demands of home-country regulators. As we shall see in the following section, the perceptions of the managers we interviewed was that *guanxi* practice was simply essential for establishing new business and accessing important information. In what follows, we argue that they 'split' the concept between the 'good' aspects (involving a 'normalization' discourse which drew parallels between *guanxi* and Western social networks) and the 'bad' aspects (which emphasized the dangers of corruption and bribery).

Good *guanxi*/bad *guanxi*

We interviewed 40 Western managers about their experiences of using *guanxi* (see Methodological Appendix for further details). Many of those interviewed about this topic (n=28) emphasized the changes that occurred as part of the government's drive to reduce the influence of *guanxi* in business operations. They framed this move in terms of a desire by the Chinese government to encourage the banking system to converge on international business norms. One CEO described the current environment in the following way:

> In China today, what we see is that there are such levels of paranoia at the top levels of government to be viewed as not being influenced by this [*guanxi*]. That in some way it hurts their national image and what they really want is to be seen as a good and reliable global citizen.
>
> (Interviewee #10)

Another aspect of the 'normalization' discourse could be found among managers who drew parallels between Western social networking and Chinese *guanxi*. For example, one manager noted that:

> People say to me, explain to me about *guanxi* and I say, well, you've got some mates, haven't you? How do you use that network? It's the same thing. *Guanxi* exists everywhere; everybody uses *guanxi* connections, business networks, that kind of thing. There's nothing strange or unusual about that.
>
> (Interviewee #3)

However, while acknowledging similarities between *guanxi* and Western social networks, managers used a good/bad dichotomy to define their *guanxi* encounters. 'Bad' *guanxi* refers to acts of reciprocity which could be defined as corruption. Recalling an encounter with an official who wanted special terms for a personal loan, one representative officer noted:

> There are good and bad *guanxi*. Bad *guanxi* can mean that you do business with people that you shouldn't do business with. The corrupt *guanxi* because you have to pay them. Good *guanxi* means that you commit yourself and you have a long-term view … but corruption is the bad *guanxi* in China. The bad *guanxi* here is a terrible thing and it's still around and that is one of the dangers to the system.
>
> (Interviewee #32)

However, the managers also understood the importance of local *guanxi* networks for operating effectively in China. They defined the term positively in relation to its similarity to general social networking and acknowledged its importance for developing and maintaining legitimate working relationships. As we shall see below, the way in which managers discussed their networking strategies shows some interesting variations and demonstrates the creative ways in which actors respond to their institutional context.

Long-termism and commitment

Perhaps the most obvious strategy for developing good networks with local officials can be seen in the group of 12 managers who said that they had relied on the networks of their senior-level Chinese staff who had already established long-term relationships with officials. As a commercial banking manager noted:

> My deputy, who has been 18 years in this bank, has a very good network of good and interesting and important contacts in China from which we benefit from enormously. You have to get contacts at different levels, because that's the way to open doors in China. You need an understanding of the way things are organised, delegated and authorised and so on. And she absolutely has that in the regulatory circles.
>
> (Interviewee #1)

Managers in this group were also particularly keen to emphasize that they were part of a company which had well-established, long-term and high-quality relationships with senior-level Chinese state officials. This was justified through reference to the trading history of the company and, interestingly, through reference to the quality of negotiations which had been made by their own home-based politicians at the national governmental level. In this group, there was an attempt to underscore their home government's low-key and supportive engagement with the Chinese government. As one manager noted:

> We have a very good reputation in China, we don't engage in China bashing which might happen in other countries in the West. Although we criticise we don't do it publicly and they appreciate that and respect us for it.
>
> (Interviewee #38)

Justification for network-building in this group is largely driven by a legitimacy-seeking narrative. The emphasis on establishing and maintaining networks with officials is nested in a discourse surrounding 'long-term commitment'. This is not a unique finding, or in any sense unexpected, as this kind of strategy has been found in other studies (Park & Luo, 2001; Tung & Worm, 2001). It is theoretically interesting in the context of this study, however, because it shows the way in which managers seek to establish legitimacy by reference to the need for 'commitment' in network-building. More importantly, it deliberately steers clear of reference to the more nuanced use of *guanxi* in terms of a culturally specific form of favour exchange (or *guanxi* practice), which prioritizes the advancement of personal objectives over adherence to formal rules.

Opportunists, ambiguous preferences and 'bending the rules'

Another way in which networks with officials were developed was through hiring individuals who had been recommended by the officials themselves. Managers in this group were keen to justify their actions through emphasizing that any employee recruited through this channel must also demonstrate sufficient skills and abilities to proceed through a standardized recruitment process. A regional chief operating officer noted that while he was 'open to suggestions' from officials, the candidate must also show some aptitude for the post:

> We always do get asked though, by people of influence, whether we would consider taking so and so … And yes, I've done that. I've hired people from the regulators' offices and I know that doesn't do us any harm, but they've got to go through a formal process. There is one young bloke who's the mayor's son in [Chinese city]. He's a bright young bloke and he's a good lad. But I know it gives us a lot of brownie points because we've actually got the mayor's son in here.
>
> (Interviewee #18)

Indeed, all in this group were keen to note that political connections alone were not enough to validate making an appointment. Methodologically, we would not necessarily expect anyone to openly admit otherwise in an interview situation; however, as we shall see below, some participants were prepared to disclose controversial experiences. To some extent, however, it also reflects the way in which managers felt obliged to conform to home-country recruitment policies. Several of our participants expressed frustration with the perceived 'interference' of headquarter human resources (HR) managers in this regard because they felt they were too distant from the situation. One relationship manager noted:

> The HR lady comes out, she meets these people and she says, 'I don't know if I can trust them'. She thinks, 'I'm here to protect our company', but she just doesn't get it, it's too hard for her to understand how things work here.
>
> (Interviewee #2)

Overall, however, it is not surprising that senior managers seek to justify their actions through balancing their need to develop informal contacts with officials with an acknowledgement that due regard is paid to the standardized norms of recruitment based on a candidate's skills and experience. As actors centred between two different networks, they are influenced by two, sometimes contradictory, sets of ideas. It is possible, in effect, to think of two different 'logics' influencing the perceptions among managers in this group. First, there is an attempt to maintain a 'logic of legitimacy' which emphasizes meritocratic hiring based on head office expectations that recruitment follows standardized formal processes of advertising, interviewing and selection based on relevant skills and experience. Second, there is a 'logic of appropriateness', given that in this particular context there is a very real practical need to hire people who are recommended by local officials because it helps to raise the profile of the bank in regulatory circles. Our participants coupled an official discourse of employee skill and formal recruitment practices with a willingness to engage with the norms of the local environment through entering reciprocal relationships with local officials. In an ambiguous situation, those who are 'opportunists' may flourish by redeploying the existing cultural and institutional rules to their own ends.

Another strategy actively used by our 'opportunists' was to directly cultivate informal networks with local officials, rather than through a connection. Here, the manager sought to provide a range of services to an individual with regulatory influence on the presumption that this would be reciprocated with assistance with licensing issues. This is the closest example in our sample of Western actors attempting to model instrumental *guanxi* practice. There are, of course, inherent dangers with this strategy. Given the pressure from central government to reduce reliance on personal relationships in business, some local officials were keen to exit from this kind of relationship with Western executives. As an example of this, one retail banking manager described a recent incident in relation to their attempt to acquire a bank licence:

> Well, we were having a bit of a time of it trying to get a licence in Shanghai and we had a good local government contact there who we thought could help us get things organised. But this was just after that business with Chen right, and everyone was really jittery, and he told us in no uncertain terms to get lost, which, really, was probably an over-reaction, because we weren't, strictly speaking, asking him to do anything illegal, just to perhaps help us develop our case and maybe push it to the front of the queue.
>
> (Interviewee #39)

This particular Western bank had been involved in advising the official on several financial matters and our participant felt that this had established his bank as a 'favourite' in the regulatory office. However, the official was now uneasy and refused to be drawn into favour exchange in case he was personally compromised. What we see here is an attempt to use local connections without understanding the time-limited nature of such relationships in an unstable institutional environment. Moreover, it underscores the way in which 'appropriate' action is framed by some managers according to their (perhaps misguided) perception of what is acceptable in the local context.

Another manager discussed how he had been asked by local officials to provide loan support for a construction project, a request he had complied with in order to improve his chances of receiving a bank licence, only to find that, when he approved the loan, further financial assistance was requested for a substantially riskier project.

> It can be frustrating here because the rules are not laid out explicitly. You come here and want to do something, say get a licence. And you're asked to do certain things, and you do them, and then they say, right you need to do something else now. And you do that, and then you have to do something else as well. And those 'somethings' have involved us in some exchanges which, outside of China, might be problematic. But the thing is that, here, the legal framework is still evolving so you have to give them

> time in that area and in the meantime you have to do what you have to do to get your business established.
>
> (Interviewee #24)

Rather than acknowledge the implications of their *own* actions, liability is shifted outwards so that responsibility for enforcing change is placed entirely on the shoulders of domestic actors. Western managers do not always push their Chinese partners to observe the rules and regulations as laid down by the WTO or China's own regulatory bodies. As this informant says, 'you have to give *them* time'. It is implied, therefore, that 'normal' business practice should be deferred until such a time, in the unknown future, when rational-legal processes have become well established. By transferring responsibility for change to host-country nationals, these Western managers are, in effect, contributing to the maintenance of informal circumventory *guanxi* practices, and are certainly not encouraging convergence towards international norms. In this sense, we see further confirmation of the 'problem of change' outlined earlier. There is little evidence of Western bankers driving through efficiency measures in a competitive environment. Rather, they opportunistically use the existing cultural and institutional structures to advance their own interests as best they can. While these actions may well prove insignificant in the development of rational-legal systems in China over the long term, it is important to note that it is not at all *inevitable* that China's incorporation into the international economy will lead to the displacement of such practices, not least because international managers themselves experience a process of adaptation as they conform to what they believe to be acceptable and legitimate in the local context.

Discussion

The introduction of market-orientated institutions into China, from the late 1970s onward, pitched a new institutional system against an older one. As discussed in Chapter 4, in the late 1990s, the assumption of Chinese policy-makers, such as former Premier Zhu Rongji, an eminent economic reformer, was that foreign banks, and their managers, would bring about desired change in the system because competition would increase efficiency. At the organizational level, foreign bankers could unsettle dominant practices, such as nepotistic recruitment and reward, and drive the adoption of preferred alternatives, such as meritocratic hiring and promotions (Mahoney & Thelen, 2010). In this context, Western banks were allowed entry into the Chinese market to act as *agents of change*. In other words, in line with the assumptions of Guthrie (2001), mimetic isomorphism would occur in Chinese joint venture banks and we would see the widespread adoption of the HR systems and practices used in foreign banks, as convergence occurred towards international best practice. Of course, we know that this is not what occurred in practice. A hybrid system of Chinese HRM has emerged which ensures the continuation of long-held cultural values such respect for seniority, protection of 'face', and the use of affective, sentimental *guanxi* networks (Warner, 2014a).

As we discussed in Chapter 2, the informal influences of culture and meaning can represent the most taken-for-granted assumptions about reality. For scholars such as Redding (2005), it is *culture* that generates the rules which define the framework of institutional order in a given society. Culturally embedded social interactions and networks are, therefore, relatively enduring and are less readily open to change than formal, regulatory institutions. Clearly, then, culture is key to understanding the *context* of China's banking sector. However, we would argue that the instrumental aspect of *guanxi* practice, favour exchange, is also about power relations, especially when those networks include Western bankers and Chinese officials. The ability of Westerners to form the connections they need with influential Chinese actors is influenced by what it is they can offer in the exchange process. This might include jobs for relatives or special help with loans. Either way, it has consequences for their ability to change existing institutional arrangements.

In this chapter, we have seen how some Western actors adapt to local cultural norms (as they perceive them) and, as a consequence, their behaviour reinforces the use of instrumental *guanxi* in elite power–money networks. For example, the 'opportunists' who actively pursued network alliances with influential Chinese who, in turn, may have been interested in maintaining the status quo, are in no sense 'agents of change'. In China, Western bankers are in a relatively weak position, particularly when compared with the power and influence they hold in other parts of the world. This necessarily influences their ability, and inclination, to change existing institutional arrangements. Moreover, while individual bankers may earnestly believe their use of instrumental, exchange-based *guanxi* will win new business for their firms, they may underestimate the risk this poses to their organization. As we have seen, adaptation to *perceived* local cultural norms may lead to dismissal, a criminal record and the imposition of heavy fines.

Conclusions

As discussed in Chapter 5, it is possible to identify efforts to develop a formal regulatory framework in the banking sectors which is based on a *rational-legal system*, as we would expect from Weberian theory. But, as we have demonstrated in this chapter, informal networking remains 'clannish' (Boisot & Child, 1996) and influence in the banking system is still largely organized through well-established networks based on political power. We would agree strongly that *cultural* context is indeed important for understanding Chinese management practice and that *guanxi* is enduring, in all its forms (Bian 2018; Warner, 2014c).

Our contribution here has been to extend the notion of 'context' beyond culture by drawing attention to the power relations that exist between Western managers and Chinese officials. These networks might have strong cultural roots, but they are largely based on an instrumental form of *guanxi* practice grounded in favour exchange. Instrument *guanxi* is the only form likely to be available to Western bankers, and few will be drawn into the affective, sentiment-derived *guanxi* ties based on kinship or friendship connections. We would argue that these instrumental forms of networking may lack the emotional qualities of benevolence and courtesy more commonly found in affective *guanxi* and may rely more on coercion (Barbalet, 2017). Indeed, as we will see in the following chapter, Western bankers struggle to establish trusting relationships with their Chinese counterparts and may be framed as tricksters who are a threat to economic security.

8 The 2008 financial crisis and trust relationships between Chinese and Western bankers

In this chapter, we examine how the 2008 financial crisis influenced levels of confidence and trust between Western and Chinese bankers. We begin by briefly outlining the key cultural features of trust relationships in China before moving on to discuss the reputation of Western banks in China prior to the 2008 financial crisis. We present a variety of perspectives on whether Western investors could be trusted with the task of assisting reforms in Chinese banks. Next, we turn to our interview data and analyze the views of Chinese managers on the perceived trustworthiness of their Western partners. We also draw on interviews with our Western managers to describe the day-to-day practices they encountered when in low-trust relationships with Chinese partners. Finally, we examine the reputational damage suffered by Western banks following the sub-prime crisis and analyze the consequences of this for business relationships in China.

Trust relationships in China

As discussed in earlier chapters, deep *guanxi* networks based on trusted kin connections and long-standing friendships can provide a reliable support structure in an unstable institutional environment (Yang, 2002; Bian, 2018). An enduring lack of confidence in the rational-legal framework means that China's 'network capitalism' is unlikely to disappear anytime soon (Nolan, Rowley & Warner, 2016). Tightly linked social and business networks continue to guide individual decision-making and trust relationships in what Boisot and Child (1996) labelled the 'iron law of fiefs'. Moreover, Confucian principles based on honouring established seniority and maintaining harmonious relationships in social groups can make it difficult for outsiders to establish trusting relationships (Warner, 2014b). Social psychological studies have shown that trust is usually highly dependent on strong in-group and out-group distinctions, and managers from collectivist cultures, such as China, may have a stronger in-group bias than those from 'individualist' cultures (Watkins & Liu, 1996; Yamagashi, Cook & Watabe, 1998). This, in turn, may lead to a lower individual propensity to trust external partners in business relationships (Huff & Kelley, 2003).

Of course, the notion that social trust in China is a uniform outcome based on a Confucian cultural heritage, embedded in an unreliable institutional framework, does not fully capture the complexity of the process, where change can be rapid and vary from region to region (Zhang & Ke, 2003). This view has been amplified more recently by Zhai (2017) who notes: 'Given that Chinese cultural traditions are complex and multi-dimensional, it is ineffective to deal with this notion by a single index' (Zhai, 2017, p. 1). Nevertheless, in societies where mistrust of non-kin relationships is high (such as in China, Korea, Italy and France) trust in both outsiders and formal institutions may tend to be low (Fukuyama, 1995). For Fukuyama, China is a 'low trust society' largely because of the continuing influence of Confucian values, which he defines as 'the elevation of family bonds above all other social loyalties'. He argues that the level of 'familism' encountered in China may create a 'deficit of trust among people not related to one another' (Fukuyama, 1995, p. 29). We will demonstrate aspects of this phenomenon in our interviews below, but we will first consider other factors that influence trust relationships in business, such as institutional credibility and reputation.

The reputation of Western banks prior to the 2008 financial crisis

As discussed in Chapter 4, the rationale for opening Chinese banks to foreign investment rested on a belief that the systems operating in Western banks were likely to bring greater efficiencies to Chinese banks. During the late 1990s and early 2000s, there was a clearly identifiable group of influential officials who trusted the operating systems of Western banks and were open to 'learning from the West' in terms of economic development (Zhang, 2017). In this sense, Western banks were held in high esteem and were perceived to be credible, influential institutions. Bourdieu (2005) argues that these characteristics are essential elements of the *symbolic capital* of any organization and are crucial to developing trust relationships. In terms of our case study, the symbolic capital of Western banks was high in the early reform period because of their perceived competencies and international reputation. Some officials, such as Wang Qishan and Zhu Rongji, had argued that foreign investors could change the ownership structure of Chinese banks and reduce the problems of 'moral hazard' associated with the monobank system (Paulson, 2015; Wong, 2016). More importantly, for the purposes of this chapter, a high level of trust was placed in the *capability* of foreign owners to introduce new management ideas. As CBRC (2005) noted:

> Through sending people to sit on the boards of senior management of the local banks and bringing into play their advantages in the areas of legal awareness, professional ethics, specific skills and management expertise, the strategic investors may help the local banks improve their corporate governance, internal controls, information disclosure and financial management … In addition, the cooperation between the overseas strategic

> investors and the local banks [may] also … involve the areas of … organizational restructuring, IT system design, marketing, customer relationships, product development (e.g. credit card, wealth management, and consumer credit products), risk control techniques and risk management systems, performance assessment and so on.

In brief, Chinese policy-makers trusted Western banking practices and believed that an association with these institutions would improve the reputation and credibility of local banks.

The 'New Left' perspective: financial security and economic colonization

While influential officials thought the path to financial stability lay in developing partnerships with foreign banks, others saw them as fundamentally untrustworthy and a threat to China's economic sovereignty. Some members of the so-called 'New Left' thinkers had been highly critical of China's economic reforms, arguing that China should return to Maoist-style centrally planned economic system (Freeman & Yuan, 2011). A sub-group of the 'New Left' was extremely hostile to the foreign ownership of Chinese banks (Naughton, 2006). For example, Yu Yunhui (of Debang Securities) and Luo Deming (of the Bank of Shanghai) are quoted as arguing that the banking sector was far too important to sell to foreigners, even in minority shareholdings. Selling bank shares, they argued, would amount to 'economic colonization, "Latin Americanization", and loss of economic sovereignty' (Naughton, 2006, p. 5). Writing in *Yinghangjia zazhi* (The Banker Magazine) in 2005, Yu and Luo emphasized the need to remember the predatory nature of Western banks:

> A top executive of Hong Kong and Shanghai Bank gazed at the Bank of Communications Tower in Pudong and said: 'It won't be long before the name of the Bank of Communications Tower is changed to the Hong Kong and Shanghai Bank Tower'. Stealthily controlling Ping'an Insurance, gaining control of the Bank of Communications, then controlling a securities company, a fund management company, and finally completing the setup of a comprehensive financial trust company in China, this is the strategy of the foreign 'strategic investors' such as Hong Kong and Shanghai Bank.
>
> (Naughton, 2006, p. 5)

They go on to argue that such a situation would be a 'blueprint for financial domination by foreign banks' (Naughton, 2006, p. 5). The alternative, Leftists suggested, was to open up the state-owned banks to China's own private sector. They argued that there would be no advantage in having foreign strategic investors because, given that their underlying plan was to dominate the Chinese market, they would be unlikely to reveal their 'secrets' anyway. The debate became particularly heated when Chinese bank stocks that were sold to foreign investors increased rapidly in value following their IPOs. One widely discussed example was Bank of America's acquisition of 10% of the China Construction Bank in 2005 for $3 billion (Naughton, 2006). Following the end of the lock-up period in 2009, Bank of America sold its initial investment for $12.9 billion which led to a hostile reaction among the New Leftists and sections of the Chinese media (He & Ping, 2014). The perception was that the stocks had been sold far too cheaply in the first place and that, once again, the Chinese had been exploited by predatory Western capitalists (He & Ping, 2014). However, defenders of the policy argued that the only reason that the price increased in value following the IPO was because of the inclusion of such high-profile foreign investors (Naughton, 2006). Prior to the IPO, several banking scandals had erupted and two heads at the Bank of Construction were charged with criminal misconduct. These incidents significantly increased Bank of America's negotiating power. Finally, when Citibank, one of the Chinese government's preferred partners, actually withdrew from the bidding process altogether, Bank of America used every problem with the Chinese banking system, including corruption scandals, government interference and uncertified accounts, to drive down the price of the shares prior to the IPO (Naughton, 2006). The Bank of America certainly did drive a hard bargain in the pre-IPO negotiations, but, in the early days, the Chinese banks were an unknown quantity to the international markets. Bank of America was taking a risk by getting involved with the Bank of Construction and its international reputation, at the time, no doubt contributed to the successful IPO. In sum, however, the debate about selling banks, shares to foreign investors highlights the long-standing arguments in China's own intellectual community about whether Western banks were an important source of new management ideas and banking technologies, or, alternatively, whether they were an inherent threat to China's financial security (see Bickers, 2017). Suffice to say, we saw that many of these themes resonated with the Chinese managers we interviewed. As highly educated and active members of the business community, they had followed the debates on the relative merits of working with Western banks and referred to them as they described their experiences.

Cheating, tricking and lack of respect

In our interviews with Chinese managers, the first theme that we encountered was the strong belief that they were vulnerable to being 'tricked' and 'cheated' by foreign bankers. The second theme which emerged from the data related to a perceived lack of cultural sensitivity among the Western expatriates they encountered in the workplace. Taken together, it should come as no surprise to find that their experiences had been largely negative and rested on an assumption that Western bankers were not trustworthy.

Cheating and tricking

Our Chinese participants were asked to focus their discussions on experiences of working with a foreign partner, overseas director or technical expert. While they were given the opportunity to focus on positive aspects of the working relationship, all described problems which could be linked to a lack of trust in their Western colleagues. These related to threats to proprietary information and the broader issue of financial security. For example, one Chinese manager spoke of his experiences of working in a joint-venture investment banking scheme which, at the time of interview, was on the verge of collapse. From his perspective, the crisis had arisen because of attempts by the foreign partner to steal data from the Chinese bank and use it to develop their own client list. As he observed:

> It might seem to the outside that it isn't working because of the business reasons but it is actually because of the financial security reasons. They are trying to set up a separate company and use the data from us. So they say to the media it's just because of the business differences, but that's not so.
>
> (Interviewee #43)

All of the Chinese managers interviewed for this study (n=20) made much of the fact that while Western bankers were indeed highly skilled, they still felt threatened by their presence in China and were suspicious of their intentions. As one Chinese investment banker noted:

> Levels of trust are very low, from the Chinese banking side anyway, and the higher you go then the more true that is. They are our competitors. Yes, sure we might like to get their advice but we will make up our own mind and we will definitely not let them cheat us.
>
> (Interviewee #56)

On occasion there was a perceived power imbalance between the two parties and this created a sense of insecurity among the Chinese managers who felt vulnerable and open to exploitation. A senior Chinese manager, then working in a large American bank, recalled his time in negotiations over the establishment of a joint-venture bank:

> So, you have this asymmetry of power and information which goes in favour of the foreign expert. We're not as sophisticated as them and that's an underlying truth. And there are many cases we know of where they didn't fully disclose the complexity of the risk of a deal to you. So you are put in a position where you are not as sophisticated as your counterparts and you are disadvantaged, because, actually, they really do know more and because of that they may want to trick you.
>
> (Interviewee #62)

In this example, an information asymmetry had created feelings of insecurity and mistrust in the intentions of the Western partner. Moreover, given the historical record of exploitation by Western actors in China, it is understandable that some Chinese managers may express low levels of trust in their interpersonal interactions. Despite public statements which emphasize the advantages of co-operation, we should not forget that Chinese and Western banks are ultimately in competition for China's financial market.

Lack of respect

As well as the theme of 'cheating and tricking', a related view was that Western expatriate staff who had been sent to work in the banks lacked personal credibility. More specifically, this seemed to relate to the absence of senior people 'working on the ground' with Chinese colleagues. One Chinese executive described his frustration with an American bank which sent young (under 35) Harvard MBAs to work on collaborative projects. He described the situation as follows:

> I have problems dealing with US colleagues in Shanghai, they think they know China well, they think they understand the facts here. But they think about our behaviours based on their own understanding. They think they can be on the same level with me. Traditionally, Chinese think senior people have more experience, but also that they have all the right relationships with people in all the right channels, so they have good interpersonal skills and they know how to build relationships with people. Young people can't do this.
>
> (Interviewee #55)

Others noted that while some foreign technical experts may even have excellent Mandarin language skills, they still lacked sufficient cultural experience and sensitivity to engage effectively with Chinese colleagues. One Chinese informant noted:

> Even though he [Western manager] spoke fluent Mandarin and had many years' experience in Asia, he still does not correctly understand Chinese culture or Chinese people. He expected too much from us, he was too impatient and did not speak to us correctly.
>
> (Interviewee #46)

Certainly, one of the common themes among the Chinese managers concerned their views on the importance of the *seniority* of the foreign delegation that was sent to work in China. The view here was that the networks of more senior managers would inevitably be more powerful and useful than those of a younger person. As one general manager noted:

> In China, if you want to get a big project, or an underwriting project, then for the very basic issues, yes, you can send the young people to do that, but it must be a President who meets with us to make the real decisions. Why? Because it is clear that they have the good relationships in government and financial circles. Those foreigners who do it well here are those who take their time and send their most senior people, they get the rewards.
>
> (Interviewee #50)

Indeed, there were numerous examples of Chinese managers (n=13) who simply insisted on dealing with senior Western financiers over the period we studied. In an institutional environment permeated with low levels of trust in foreign partners, seniority could help establish at least some level of credibility. This related to a belief that a senior person had important connections, but also that sending a senior person to build relationships indicated due regard for the *prestige* associated with such relationships. One Chinese executive who had worked on several joint ventures noted that on each occasion he had been greatly concerned about this and offered the following view:

> We wanted to know who they could deliver in terms of seniority. Some guys can send the President, and those who did that got the deal. If they can get that kind of support it works, it shows us seriousness and actually that they respect us.
>
> (Interviewee #61)

All of this draws our attention to the importance of cultural aspects of interpersonal trust such as face, or *mianzi*, in the Chinese business context (see Chapter 2 for further discussion). A person's 'face' is often perceived to be determined by their occupational position and organizational affiliation which, in turn, impacts the 'quality' of their network through associated levels of power and money (Park & Luo, 2001). These factors further highlighted the specific nature of symbolic capital in China, namely the crucial importance placed on reputation and credibility in establishing trusting relationships. In China, a trusting relationship may become stronger if one's partner is perceived to be someone with superior connections (Park & Luo, 2001). In this regard, Western bankers sometimes failed to establish trusting relationships because they did not convince their Chinese co-workers that they were a 'respectable' or influential individual. Indeed, the perception was that those who had been sent to support technical assistance projects (as opposed to higher-level strategic advisors) were disappointing and lacked the cultural and social skills necessary to succeed.

Practices used in low-trust interactions

Chinese executives used diverse strategies to defend against the perceived predatory intentions of foreign banks. In the following section, we focus mainly (though not exclusively) on the actions of Chinese managers as reported to us by our Western participants. While our Chinese participants were prepared to discuss their relationships with Western partners, they were understandably less open to revealing the day-to-day practices they used in order to advance their own interests. The sources of regulatory obstruction that were experienced by Western banks were discussed at length in Chapter 5. Here, we outline the other informal difficulties Western bankers faced in their daily operations. These included: (i) last-minute demands that senior members of the board be changed after those individuals had been approved (n=5 reported events); (ii) requests that employees at locally incorporated Western banks take 'tests' which, on further enquiry, did not seem to exist (n=6 reported events); (iii) pressures from Chinese partners to publish sensitive corporate information (n=8 reported events); (iv) 'hostile' flash auditing (n=20 reported events); and (v) initiating new partnerships without consultation (n=28 reported events). In relation to the practice of flash auditing, one Western executive described his experience as follows:

> It's actually been quite aggressive. They sent in scores of auditors and they were there for weeks. This wasn't in any way a standard professional audit. We think they were there to raid data actually – they claim they wanted to be absolutely sure we were following their procedures, but I've never seen anything like it. I think a lot of it is to do with the regulators becoming more nationalistic, more aggressive towards us.
>
> (Interviewee# 38)

Indeed, this perception of increased 'nationalism' and aggression was a consistent theme among our Western participants. Several described it in terms of a drift away from the influence of Western ideas. One vice president noted:

> In China, we're seeing a clear movement towards tradition, not towards the West. When I was here in the 1990s, all the young people wanted to learn from the Americans, the Brits. They wanted to go to London, or Harvard or Stanford. Now less and less people want to go to the US and UK. I think there's a recognition that this is their country, their culture, their way of doing things … more and more graduates want to work in SOEs. In the 1990s no graduate would want to do that.
>
> (Interviewee #48)

Participants also reported ways in which individual branches had been targeted. For example, one Western manager reported that the police had visited a local branch which had recently opened and requested that the vault be changed, even though it met the required standards as described in their initial permission documents. The branch was closed immediately and was not allowed to re-open for some days during which time local rumours circulated that the foreign bank was not a 'safe' place to deposit money.

> That whole thing just trashed our reputation. There was nothing wrong with our systems, nothing wrong with our procedures and certainly nothing wrong with our vault. We did everything by the book and there was in no way a security problem in that branch. But they simply didn't want us in town and they made damn sure they did their best to ruin our reputation and get us out of there.
>
> (Interviewee #49)

When asked why he thought this had happened, the manager mentioned that the local police chief was related to a Chinese banker with whom he had once tried to develop a business relationship. The proposed deal had gone wrong and had ended with bad feeling on both sides. The manager observed:

> The situation here is that they (the Chinese banking community) resent us, they dislike us. Yes, there's all that stuff about learning from each other but scratch the surface and you'll see that many really can't stand us. They've learnt their history in a certain way and their belief is that we cannot be trusted. They see us as dangerous and threating. Like wolves. The West have always tried to exploit the Chinese, so why should we be any different to our own ancestors?
>
> (Interviewee #49)

A lack of trust between business partners can mean that a commitment to maintaining a relationship is damaged (Das & Teng, 1998; Meier et al., 2016). We found evidence of this among our own participants. One of the most widely reported practices used by Chinese managers was the initiation of new deals which technically breached the initial 'agreement' with the Western partner. One senior Chinese manager outlined his suspicions about the intentions of his foreign partner in a 'co-operation agreement' and discussed how this had led him to look for alternatives:

> Our relationship with them is like this: we are in a co-operation agreement with them and they have two members on our board. But the relationship is not a good relationship because they are trying to change and control us, not help us. We want them to help us – with card development in particular – not to try and rule us.
>
> (Interviewee #59)

This lack of trust in the original Western partner led him to initiate a co-operation agreement with another foreign bank. This, unsurprisingly, led to significant tension with the original partner. Given the tenuous legal status of 'co-operation agreements' in China, the original partner had very little control over this decision. As our informant elaborated:

> Currently we're working on consumer cards. Now, during the project, some state-owned companies said: 'We want to have corporate cards, how about that? You work with cards right?' But they [American Bank] wouldn't help us, they said: 'Well this doesn't fit in with our strategic direction.' So we set up a parallel project with [European Bank] and they got very angry about this. But why did they get so angry? They know about cards but they won't help us. Right now, there's a real lack of trust between us, because we know they have a hidden agenda. They only want to do consumer cards so they can get to our retail customers anyway. They know if the state-owned companies get in on this then they'll have no chance of getting at that market.
>
> (Interviewee #59)

In sum, low levels of trust between Chinese and Western partners created many difficulties in day-to-day operations. If Western banks had any symbolic capital in China, it was because of their international reputation, and for many that was severely tarnished by the 2008 financial crisis.

The 2008 financial crisis: damage to the esteem and reputation of Western banks

As discussed earlier, those hostile to the introduction of Western banks were not convinced that their entry to the market would do anything to improve the profitability of Chinese banks. This was partly due to the perception that Western banks were less likely to make long-term commitments to building a business relationship (Naughton, 2006). Luo Ping, the Deputy Director-General of the CBRC's international department, was quoted in 2006 as saying: 'foreign investors' penchant for short-term gains undermines long-term business investment and the country's growth potential' (Ho, 2006). As the catastrophic consequences of the financial crisis of 2008 began to unfold, Ping's comments received some verification. A number of key Western banks found themselves in a particularly vulnerable position just at the time when their three-year lock-in period to Chinese banks expired. Given the significant increase in the value of Chinese bank shares, unwinding these investments to recapitalize their own banks appeared like a very attractive option, despite the damage it might cause to their reputation in China. Table 8.1 lists the Western banks who sold a significant amount of their Chinese investments during the financial crisis.

In April 2009, American Express and Allianz each sold approximately half their stakes in ICBC, netting a collective $1.9 billion (Kwok & Flaherty, 2009). Goldman Sachs also began to sell shares in ICBC in 2009 and sold all remaining shares in 2013 with gross proceeds from the sales amounting to around $10.1 billion (Lau & Barreto, 2013). In August 2011, Bank of America made $8.3 billion from a share sale in CCB, and a further $1.8 billion in January 2012 (Baretto & Rudegeair, 2013).

Table 8.1 Foreign bank share divestment (February 2009)

Foreign bank divestments
American Express Co. divesting shares in ICBC
Allianz SE divesting shares in ICBC
Bank of America Corporation divesting shares in China Construction Bank
Royal Bank of Scotland Group plc divesting shares in Bank of China Ltd
UBS selling its entire stake in Bank of China
Goldman Sachs selling 20% of its stake in ICBC

Sources: Barreto & Rudegeair, 2013; Kwok & Flaherty, 2009; Lau & Barreto, 2013.

As discussed in Chapter 5, Chinese banks themselves were largely shielded from the financial crisis because they had limited exposure to complex financial products, such as derivatives. However, they did still incur some loses and according to figures released by the SASAC, companies directly controlled by the state recorded book loses from investments in derivatives of $1.7 billion by the end of October 2008 ('Goldman Sachs', 2010). Although not a huge amount when compared with global banking losses, the event served to reinforce existing beliefs about the unreliability of Western banks among certain key Chinese officials. Li Wei, Deputy Chair of the SASAC in 2008, was openly critical of derivatives products and Western investment banks. Writing in the *Study Times*, a newspaper published by the school of the Communist Party's Central Committee, Li noted that derivatives bought by Chinese banks from Merrill Lynch, Morgan Stanley and Citigroup had caused some serious problems ('Chinese Official Raps', 2009). Although he acknowledged that the Chinese companies themselves held some responsibility for their losses, his key complaint was the nature of the financial products developed by Western banks:

> Some international investment banks are the biggest villains … Of course, we need to find problems in the [Chinese] companies themselves … But it is also largely related to international investment banks maliciously peddling high-leverage, complex products with fraudulent characteristics.
>
> ('Chinese Official Raps', 2009)

Li also stressed that his agency would support any company who wished to challenge contracts with Western investment banks through the court system. Li's comments are among the most critical comments that were publicly made by Chinese officials about the financial crisis. The crisis confirmed the suspicions of those on the political left who had been sceptical about the intentions and competencies of Western banks in the first place. The public use of language such as 'villains' and 'fraudulent' by a high-level government minister in official publications indicates that the credibility and symbolic capital of some Western banks disintegrated rapidly in the post-2008 period. Indeed,

Former US Treasury Secretary, Hank Paulson, recalled a meeting with Wang Qishan, Vice Premier in charge of China's financial and economic affairs in 2008. Paulson had been arguing that China should open up its banking system to more foreign competition, to which Wang replied: 'You were my teacher but look at your system, Hank, we aren't sure we should be learning from you anymore' (Paulson, 2015, p. 178)

Irrelevant and no longer needed: the IPO of the Agricultural Bank of China

Further evidence of the diminishing influence of Western banks comes from a study of the IPO for the Agricultural Bank of China (ABC). In July 2010, the ABC became the last of China's 'Big Four' policy banks to go public. ABC was the biggest of China's policy banks with 320 million retail customers, 2.7 million corporate clients, nearly 24,000 branches and $1 trillion in deposits (Wines, 2010). The key difference between this IPO and those of the other major SOBs (ICBC, CCB and BOC) was that no attempt was made to engage a foreign strategic investor *prior* to the IPO. While a certain number of foreign investors were invited to become 'cornerstone investors', including Standard Chartered and Roosbank, they were not given the heavily discounted options seen in earlier IPOs (Pei, 2010). Indeed, in the ABC deal, the largest foreign investor to sign a 'memorandum of understanding' was the Middle Eastern sovereign wealth fund, Qatar Holding, which invested $2.8 billion in the bank (Pei, 2010). This could be seen as an indicator of the diminishing financial power of Western banks in the post-crisis period. In the earlier IPOs, Chinese banks had needed the support of a well-known Western strategic investor to enhance their own credibility and improve investor confidence. However, post-2008, the reputations of many Western banks were weakened and offered little in the way of prestige to the ABC deal. Moreover, those on the political left in China were once again arguing that Western banks had never really had any significant impact in the earlier IPOs of Chinese banks. As the *China Economic Review* reported:

> The foreign banks offered to help with risk management systems and balance sheets, but their assistance had little impact. ABC may find that a better way lies in simply passing on outside help. Pursuing only domestic investors would lower the risk of management and cultural clashes, and may be more likely to produce a partner with a strong financial position able and willing to remain invested in the bank for the long term.
>
> ('Eyes on the Home Front', 2009)

Moreover, the mass sell-off by Western investors of their stakes in Chinese banks (see Table 8.1) had been taken as further evidence of the increasing 'irrelevance' of foreign strategic investors. Some Chinese commentators argued that Chinese banks had now gained a sufficient international reputation in their own right and no longer needed to rely on outsiders to enhance their standing. Guo Tianyong, a professor of finance, was quoted in the *China Daily* as saying:

> Foreign partnership used to be an endorsement for Chinese lenders to boost investor confidence, but now it has become less necessary as Chinese lenders have gained international recognition and credibility.
>
> (Bo, 2010)

This growing confidence was reflected in ABCs preparation for the IPO. The bank had much stricter requirements for foreign investors than had been the case in earlier IPOs. For instance, not only did ABC require any investing bank to specialize in rural banking, they also required that the investing bank must have 'clean and strong financial records', a requirement which, at the time, excluded many US and European banks ('Eyes on the Home Front', 2009). Reflecting on how his company's IPO compared with that of its peers, Pan Gongsheng, ABC's Vice President, noted that the earlier IPOs had faced a market where investors knew little about Chinese banks other than that they had recently been on the brink of insolvency. Optimistically, he noted that ABC 'enjoys a good reputation worldwide. So there is no need to introduce strategic banks to gain investor confidence' ('Meet Pan Gongsheng', 2010). This is indeed a bold statement given that ABC had carried the largest non-performing loan ratio of the Big Four banks. In 2006, auditors found \$7.5 billion in corrupt deals at ABC, and, in 2008, non-performing loans accounted for almost a quarter of the bank's assets. This led to a government bailout of \$19 billion and to the state purchase of around \$120 billion in bad loans prior to the IPO (Wines, 2010). However, Pan Gongsheng's optimism about ABC was vindicated by the result of the IPO which saw the stock sell for a total of \$19.2 billion. This not only ranks as one of the world's largest ever IPOs, but also led to a valuation of the bank as a whole of around \$128 billion, more than Citigroup or Goldman Sachs at the time (Wines, 2010). The ABC IPO marked a change in the fortunes of large Chinese banks, and their lack of interest in the involvement of Western banks indicated that the influence of the latter was much diminished.

Conclusion

Historically, the international esteem and reputation of Western banks had endowed them with a high level of symbolic capital. The 2008 banking crisis saw many of them stripped of that status. In this chapter, we have seen that levels of trust between Chinese and Western bankers were low and this problem was rooted in both cultural and institutional factors. While convinced that Chinese banks must change their internal systems and, ultimately, their organizational culture, some Chinese commentators have argued that the practicalities of realizing that ambition through co-operation with Western banks is extremely difficult. In an interview cited by Hawes and Chiu (2012, p. 12), the Vice-Chair of CBRC, Tang Shuangning, noted:

> After foreign strategic investors are brought in, can they really help to reform and improve the Chinese banking system? Will their new systems really be accepted by staff and become normal practice in China? It will take a very long time and require a huge effort. How to go from the outward forms of corporate governance to their substance and modify the traditional Chinese habit of placing personal relationships before impersonal systems – this is going to be an enormous problem!

Moving to the period beyond the 2008 financial crisis, it should come as no surprise that some Chinese bankers were now even less convinced of the utility of working with Western institutions. Anthony Lok, Head of Research at Hong Kong-based BOC International was quoted in *Euromoney* magazine as saying:

> Foreign banks never had much influence on Chinese banks, and Chinese banks generally were very annoyed at how useless, unwilling and unable the foreign banking partner was to help … Today [China's banks] look at 'Western bankers' and we have to think … Jeez are those guys that smart after all, or were all their lectures about excellent risk management just more bovine manure? The days of lecturing from Mount Sinai about how much better the Western financial system was ended with the collapse of Lehman Brothers and most of the Western Banking system.
>
> (Wilson, 2010, p. 37)

Following the 2008 financial crisis, China's regulators and bankers are now more assertive and many believe that the 'rules of the game' have changed significantly in their favour.

To conclude, we can observe that at the start of the banking reform process, Western banks held a high degree of symbolic capital. They had proven successes in risk assessment procedures, technical expertise in a range of financial products and, initially at least, the international reputations that the Chinese banks needed to gain a foothold in the international markets. Chinese banks, on the other hand, were able to offer social and economic capital to Western investors in the form of access to branch networks, huge numbers of customers and assistance with navigating the political landscape in China. In Bourdieu's (2005) use of the term, 'capital' comes in a variety of forms but each, in principle, can be traded for another and may allow the bearer to wield power in a given social field. As we have argued throughout this book, power is dynamic and circulates through the banking system, and the gain or loss of valued forms of capital will be associated with the ability to exercise power within and between organizations.

It was certainly possible to identify a public narrative based on the possibility of mutual co-operation between Western and Chinese banks in the early years of reform. Yet, as we have seen in this chapter, the day-to-day realities were more complex than this simple model of friendly exchange suggests. In our interviews with Chinese managers, we were able to identify a degree of mistrust towards Western bankers which was based on a fear of exploitation, as well as poor cross-cultural communication. Moreover, our Western managers identified a range of practices which they believed were aimed at subverting their chances of succeeding in the Chinese market, such as hostile flash auditing and the use of competing partnerships. On top of all these factors, many Western banks experienced significant reputational damage following the 2008 crisis. This, in turn, led Chinese policy-makers and influential business leaders to seriously question their competencies and further diminished already fragile levels of trust. Consequently, we would suggest that it will be extremely difficult for Western bankers to develop the power and influence in China that they hold in many other parts of the world.

9 Conclusions and implications

The role of Western bankers in China remains a controversial subject. For some, their enduring low profile and lack of impact are symptomatic of more fundamental problems with China's economy (Xia, 2018). Zhou Xiaochuan, the outgoing Governor of the PBC and long-standing advocate of foreign bank entry, has warned that China may be facing a 'Minsky moment', where asset values suddenly collapse and trigger a banking crisis (Kang, 2018). He argues that greater foreign competition is a necessary corrective to this risk and that 'protectionism leads to laziness' in the financial sector (Mitchell, 2017). Against this backdrop, several announcements were made throughout 2017 and 2018 that seemed to indicate that a further round of 'opening up' to foreign competition was imminent. For example, Zhu Guangyao, Vice Minister of Finance, announced that the cap on foreign investment in Chinese banks would be removed and that foreign investors would be allowed majority ownership (of 51%) in securities firms, investment managers and insurance providers (Wildau & Lockett, 2017). Furthermore, as Zhou Xiaochaun retired in 2018, it was announced that, Yi Gang, his English-speaking, US-educated protégé would take over his role as Governor of the PBC. In his maiden speech, Yi Gang promised to continue the work of his mentor, reiterating that opening up the sector to foreign investors 'leads to progress' (Yao & Zhang, 2018).

We would be cautious, however, in assuming that these announcements mark the dawn of a new era for Western banks in China. We have shown throughout this study that there is often a marked disparity between official policy announcements and the realities of institutional and organizational change. Zhou Xiaochuan faced internal resistance to his reforms for many years and, as discussed in earlier chapters, the CCP is in no way unified over such matters, with factions often competing to control the policy agenda (Galbraith & Zhou, 2017; Li, 2016; Walter, 2014). While Yi Gang's appointment in early 2018 may appear to indicate a commitment to continuing Zhou Xiaochaun's legacy of liberal-minded reforms, the political realties are more complex. As Yi Gang was promoted to the role of Governor of the PBC, Guo Shuqing, head of the China Banking and Insurance Regulatory Commission, was promoted to party secretary of the PBC. This is the first time the 'technical' and 'political' elements of the role have been split between two officers.

Observers note that this new arrangement means that Guo Shuqing has far greater political influence than Yi Gang, and his appointment as party secretary now makes him the real power in the PBC (Tang & Yu, 2018). In turn, both Yi and Guo will report to Vice Premier Liu He, a chief advisor on economic policy to President Xi Jinping. In brief, what these fresh appointments indicate is that the core CCP leadership will maintain strict control over the financial sector and Yi Gang's decision-making must be in line with the inclinations and world view of Xi Jinping himself (Mitchell, 2018). While we may witness occasional concessions towards opening up the banking sector in the coming years, we would argue that there will remain a significant degree of political ambiguity towards Western banks. This, in turn, will continue to influence the day-to-day practices of Chinese managers and officials, many of whom are already predisposed towards keeping foreign influence in check and obstructing the activities of Western banks.

We have argued throughout this study that a full understanding of the sector can only be reached by investigating the perspectives of managers themselves at the *organizational* level. Our approach assumes that business organization and economic action varies across different societies and, therefore, management practices need to be *contextualized* by reference to diverse cultures, state-influenced institutional histories and potentially conflicting perspectives on what the ultimate goal of management might be. One of our key contributions has been to use insights from organizational sociology to examine the 'below the surface' realities of the actions and influences of Western bankers in China. By doing so, we have demonstrated that *power relations* in the sector are distributed across different organizations in *dynamic* ways. This, in turn, can lead to unexpected organizational outcomes that are not easily accounted for by the conventional cultural and institutional perspectives commonly used in management studies. In the remainder of this final chapter we summarize our findings, analyze their importance and consider their implications for the study of international management more generally.

Summing up the findings

We have developed a rich, textured account based on an *interpretivist* perspective, using data gleaned through in-depth interviews conducted on-site in China with difficult-to-reach participants. We have supplemented and expanded these interviews with an analysis of relevant policy documents and media-based event data (see the Methodological Appendix for a full discussion of the strengths and limitations of our methodology). Following a comprehensive review of a diverse range of research literatures and historical sources, we identified four inter-related research objectives: (i) How does state-level policy-making influence the meaning attached to new banking regulations by different actors? (ii) Do joint ventures improve the corporate governance of Chinese banks and what kind of corporate governance structure is emerging in the sector? (iii) What role do power–money social networks play in the strategies of Western bankers at the organizational level? (iv) How did the 2008 financial crisis impact on levels of confidence and trust between Western and Chinese bankers? We summarize our theoretical arguments and key findings below.

We began Chapter 2 by questioning whether the assumptions of rational choice institutionalism can fully account for the variety of management practices that emerge in a global context. Especially popular in North American business schools, this approach often asserts that 'free' market competition improves organizational efficiencies regardless of cultural context or organizational purpose. We argued that one of the difficulties with this assumption is that, on closer inspection, few markets are 'free' from the influence of entrenched elites and regulatory capture and that different cultural values and historical circumstance create divergence in both economic action and management objectives. We demonstrated that China's banking sector is partly the legacy of the institutions of the command economy, the endurance of a well-established power-elite network and the historical memory of exploitation at the hands of the West. We argued that these factors need to be recognized when describing China's path-dependent institutional development. We also drew attention to the way in which power relations are dynamic and circulate through the banking system in ways that make straightforward collaboration between Western and Chinese bankers very difficult. There are tensions and conflicts between different kinds of bank (state-owned or foreign-owned), between banks and regulatory bodies, as well as between professional managers of different cultural backgrounds within an organization. In brief, struggles for control and dominance are not confined to the formal political sphere, but manifest in multiple ways in managers' daily organizational experiences, a theme which we identify in later chapters.

Chapter 3 outlined the *variety* of different institutions, ownership structures and product niches in the Chinese banking sector and noted that there are, as a consequence, several different kinds of business systems. The research in this study draws mainly on empirical material gathered from participants involved with banks based in the *state-owned, local corporate* and *foreign locally incorporated* systems. In other words, it is important to remember that China's banking sector is in no way homogenous and, as a consequence, we should expect day-to-day managerial practices to vary according to the particular business system in which any given bank is placed. We drew on Redding's (2005) model of comparative business systems to highlight differences between these systems, noting that societies differ in the *rationales* that underlie their economic organization. In the state-owned system, for example, banks may continue to have important policy objectives as well as profitability targets. These policy objectives may be quite specific, such as supporting large-scale government construction projects. They may, also, however, have more nuanced, politically strategic goals, such as supporting selected businesses to ensure that China continues its return to a dominant position in the global economy. These goals may sometimes conflict with those of Western investors and competitors who dismiss them as sources of inefficiencies and poor governance practices. At an organizational level, however, the consequences of these disparate goals may be the emergence of complex working relationships rooted in conflict and mistrust.

Chapter 4 presented an historical overview of the influence of Western economic ideas on the development of the banking sector in China. We focused particularly on those ideas that may influence contemporary perceptions of the utility of Western banking practices. The reasons for allowing Western banks to re-enter the market in 2007 was based on the belief that greater competition, a reduction in the extent of state ownership, and revised government regulations would help improve the efficiency of Chinese banks. It would also make managers more accountable for their decisions in the microeconomic context and thus create more rational resource allocation in the wider one. These aims grew from the technocratic reforms initiated by Premier Zhu Rongji and his followers, including Zhou Xiaochuan. These initial policy decisions regarding banks were clearly based on the core assumptions underlying rational choice economics, which was a remarkable ideological turnaround in the Chinese context, in such a short period of time. However, the move was not without its critics and there was a degree of resistance to the reforms from those on the New Left of China's political spectrum (Naughton, 2006; Freeman & Yuan, 2011). New Leftists argued that foreign banks are not to be trusted and would simply exploit China's financial sector, as they had done in the past. The chapter illustrated that Chinese politics is neither unified nor homogenous, and diverse and conflicting factions continue to influence banking regulations in many ways. China's search for global influence, we may argue, is not without its contradictions (see Warner, 2017).

At a more theoretical level, we also discussed the significance of these events for understanding institutional change and power relations in the field of Chinese banking. Based on a selective review of the historical record, foreign investors may be framed by their critics as both a threat to economic security and inherently unreliable business partners. These attitudes mean that Western banks may find themselves restricted in their activities and, as such, their ability to effect change in existing institutions has been much compromised.

Chapters 2 to 4 discussed in detail the contextual factors that influence the impact of Western banks in the Chinese banking sector. In Chapters 5 to 8 we returned to our research objectives and sought to answer those questions by drawing on our interviews with influential actors from both the Chinese and the Western banking communities. Chapter 5 investigated the question: How does state-level policy influence the meaning attached to new banking regulations by different actors, interest groups and organizations? The first part of the chapter illustrated how the Chinese regulator sought to reform domestic banks by adopting an international best-practice approach. This was achieved through, among other things, engagement with the WTO and a commitment to the Basel Accords. The appointment of high-profile foreign financial advisors to the CBRC was also an important signal to the international banking community that China was committed to regulatory reform. However, the second part of the chapter demonstrated that the regulatory structures that were actually established in China tended to favour domestic banks. We argued that the political objectives and cultural perceptions that influenced the way banking regulations developed do not neatly align with those more commonly found in the West. For example, the Anglo-Saxon corporation model usually takes profit maximization for owners and shareholders as the *raison d'être* for organizations. State regulation is often equated with government interference in the market and it is assumed that a light touch model of regulation is most likely to achieve organizational efficiencies and (assumed) profits. In China, however, this position is regarded as idiosyncratic and officials may equate the liberalization ideology with an imposition of the US experience.

We analyzed position papers published by the American Chamber of Commerce in China and the European Union Chamber of Commerce in China to track their responses to the development of new banking regulations. We observed a heavy emphasis in these documents on the inherent 'dangers' in 'protectionist' and 'discriminatory' practices, such as requiring foreign banks to move their data storage systems to mainland China. We noted, too, the tendency to use 'business case' arguments to assert that these policies would not only be impossible to implement, but would also lead to organizational inefficiencies among Chinese banks themselves. We emphazised that Anglo-Saxon 'efficiency arguments' may have limited credibility in China as they tend to overlook the role of historical memory and national identity on market development. In essence, some Chinese policy-makers remain suspicious of the motives of Western banks and it should not surprise us that, where possible, they seek to disadvantage such entities.

In Chapter 6 we considered whether joint ventures and foreign investment improved the corporate governance of Chinese banks and what kind of corporate governance model is emerging in the sector. We began by outlining the evolution of corporate governance models in different regions, highlighting the varying importance placed on shareholder and/or stakeholder models. We demonstrated that components of Western models of corporate governance, such as the Board of Directors and diversified ownership structures, have been widely adopted by Chinese banks. We then turned to our interview data to examine the system in practice. The over-riding perception of our participants was that the motivation for building strategic partnerships with Western banks was initially based on legitimacy-seeking by Chinese banks in the global financial environment. However, an enduring 'who you know' credit culture and the importance of informal cultural institutions such as *guanxi* mean that the influence of foreign banks on corporate governance reforms in China was perceived as largely ineffective. Given the serious failings of Western banks in the 2008 financial crisis, we predict that it is likely that this perception will endure in the future. At the time of writing, the Chinese 'control-based' model of corporate governance, where the state intervenes in the banking sector to ensure financial stability and to achieve social objectives, such as employment and enterprise support, is likely to endure.

Chapter 7 used in-depth interviews and case study material to investigate the question: What role do Chinese power–money social networks play in the strategies of Western bankers at the organizational level? We began by outlining the different types of *guanxi* networks in China, noting that our research focuses on instrumental and obligational ties that facilitate power–money exchanges. We showed that although there has been rapid change in the formal legislative environment, the informal normative and cultural realms are changing at a much slower pace. Indeed, *guanxi* practices may have increased in the reform period partly as a means of resisting official state and bureaucratic power. The consequence of this is that foreign banks may not, as was initially assumed in the 1990s, act as 'agents of change' in China's banking sector. Rather, they may behave opportunistically, make high-level political relationship hires, and ultimately adapt to existing institutional structures rather than actively seek to change them. After drawing on media-based event data to illustrate the problems and prospects of political relationship hires, we moved on to examine our interviews. On the one hand, the behaviour of some managers, both Chinese as well as Western, seemed to support the central government's desire to develop regulatory and business institutions that are international in form. These particular participants used the rhetoric of 'long-termism' and 'commitment' to describe the ways they build social networks in China. On the other hand, there are those whose behaviour reinforced the practice of instrumental 'favour exchange' within elite power–money networks. As a consequence, we suggest that mainstream institutional concepts such as 'isomorphism' are of limited value in explaining institutional change and stability in the Chinese context. Western bankers are now in a relatively weak position in China, especially when compared with the power and influence they wield in other parts of the world. While individual bankers may believe their networking tactics in China are beneficial to their employers, they may also underestimate the risk that such practices can bring to their organization. We showed how adaptation to the perceived cultural norms of instrumental networking may lead to heavy fines for the organization and a criminal record for the individual who may be positioned to carry the burden of punishment and reputational damage.

Chapter 8 developed these ideas further and addressed the question: How did the 2008 financial crisis influence levels of confidence and trust between Western and Chinese bankers? We began by outlining the nature of trust relationships in China and discussed the reputation of Western banks prior to the 2008 financial crisis. We then introduced conflicting perspectives on the trustworthiness of Western banks, highlighting the critique of China's New Left political movement who saw 'economic colonization' by Western banks as a real possibility. Turning to our interview data, we noted that Chinese and Western banking partnerships were often characterized by mismatched expectations. Most of the Chinese bankers we interviewed were frustrated by their interactions with Western bankers who, despite having technical expertise, were unable to engage seriously with local problems. Some were perceived as having poor cross-cultural awareness and, specifically, did not understand the importance of seniority and respectful behaviours in the workplace. At a more fundamental level, they were often perceived as 'cheaters' and as a threat to financial security, at both the organizational and institutional levels. On the other side, our Western participants reported a range of behaviours which were perceived as subverting their ability to develop their business interests. These included pressures from Chinese partners to publish sensitive corporate information, 'hostile' flash auditing by officials and the practice of initiating new partnerships without consent. Following the catastrophic banking failures of the 2008 crisis, many Western banks were stripped of their previously much-flaunted reputations and supposed technical expertise. Chinese policy-makers and bankers were less interested in what they had to offer but were also more confident in their own abilities and resources. Consequently, Western banks were shunted into ever more subordinate positions and their power and influence in China was much curtailed.

Implications of the study

Throughout this book we have demonstrated the ways in which both Chinese and Western managers construct meaning and justify practices in their daily working lives. They do so within a highly complex milieu, where there are fundamental contradictions between the operating rationales of Chinese and Western banks. Chinese management rationales, especially in the state-owned sector, are driven not only by a need to increase profitability but also by a desire to establish China as a formidable global economic power. That said, there are clearly identifiable points of conflict between New Leftists and reformers on how best to achieve this aim. Historically speaking, reformers sought to adopt international best practices and saw a clear role for foreign banks in creating competition in the sector, reducing state ownership of domestic banks and acting as models for best-practice approaches. New Leftists, however, remain resistant to these ideas and fear economic colonization. Both factions, we would suggest, are influenced by the revival of a strong nationalist sentiment and a desire to ensure China is treated with respect by its international peers. It is apparent from this observation that the ideational factors influencing management practices in China may be related to political ideologies, as well as to cultural values, which have already received so much attention in the international management research literature.

On the other hand, Western management rationales, as they relate to their operations in China, are aimed at capturing a substantial proportion of the Chinese banking market and manipulating existing institutions to their own ends. Key actors remain convinced of the superiority of their economic approaches and are convinced that Chinese banks will also best benefit through compliance with their management strategies. However, managers on the ground are also pragmatic and mindful of the need to fit in to existing cultural norms, at least as they perceive them. Thus, they attempt to ingratiate themselves within China's influential power–money networks, a move which, in itself, creates a contradiction in the assumption that they are in China to assist with the development of free market competition based on meritocratic principles. It is certainly true that, in the early 2000s, they were able to offer established competencies in a range of financial products, management systems and strategies aimed at improving governance. In some sense, at that point in time, there were clear points of alignment between their ability to provide these services and the desire of China's technocratic reformers to improve the performance of Chinese banks. However, the reputational damage sustained by Western banks during the 2008 financial crisis stripped them of much of their credibility, and they are still struggling to regain any authority. In contrast to the assumptions of some rational-choice institutionalists, we believe that there is no universal, black-box model of the firm that can be clearly targeted with standardized management systems. All the elements we have described above continue to interact with the industrialization process in China leading to diverse outcomes. If we assume that 'survival' in an institution is not just about economic success, but also about survival in its *symbolic* realm, then it should not surprise us that Western bankers struggle so much in a cultural and political milieu so different from their own.

Concluding remarks

When taken at face value, some of the management practices we have identified in this study may be described as irrational, reckless or obstructive. Yet when placed in the appropriate context, they are understandable. By turning towards a detailed investigation of contextual factors, we have gained a much deeper insight into organizational processes than we could have done by focusing on conventional indicators of economic productivity alone. At a fundamental level, we would suggest that Western bankers are not motivated by the same political goals as their Chinese counterparts. Like most foreign business people, they rarely arrive in China with anything other than a desire to make money. Indeed, their primary objectives appear to be working *within* existing institutions, rather than actively seeking to change them, as was assumed by early reformers. They simply do not have the power, or the inclination, to do otherwise.

Obtaining and adapting Western expertise has long been an important factor in China's return to global influence. However, one of the key features of the reforms, a feature many international management scholars overlook, has been resistance to any further manipulation by Western powers (Bickers, 2017; Callahan, 2014). China has a long history of using minority-share joint ventures and ownership caps as a way of protecting domestic industries from foreign competition while gaining access to foreign technologies and management expertise. Throughout this book, we have demonstrated that there is an enduring tension between the desire to acquire Western knowledge and a determination to resist further exploitation at the hands of the West. As China continues to extend itself in the global arena, we would expect to see new organizational models emerge which have been built on a unique set of cultural values, institutional histories and political ideologies. Chinese banks may well bear surface similarities to Western banks in terms of management structure and organization, but they will retain distinctive Chinese characteristics. As for the fate of Western bankers in China, we envisage that they will be restrained by a myriad of informal obstacles and will continue to play a subordinate role.

Methodological appendix

Section 1: Research strategy

When we began to plan this study, China was just beginning to open its banking sector to foreign investment and development. At that point in time, much of the previous research had focused on the manufacturing sector and we were keen to take the opportunity to investigate an entirely new area of China's economy, namely the nascent professional services. Our research agenda had developed from an interest in social networks and many of our initial ideas on how to study the reforms in the banking sector emerged from the field of organizational sociology. Given that our research position was firmly rooted in the tradition of Western social sciences, we felt that the most appropriate level of analysis for our study would be the interactions between Western and Chinese actors at the organizational level. This position was also informed by previous research on sectorial reforms in China, some of which focused on the effectiveness of joint ventures between Chinese and Western firms, and also by feasibility issues, in that we had long-standing influential contacts in the mainland who could help us develop the project. Based on our understanding of the existing research, we decided to concentrate particularly on managers' perceptions and experiences of the regulatory environment, developments in corporate governance, and the role of networking strategies and trust relationships.

There are several ways we could have researched these topics. A large-scale quantitative survey of all managers and executives in banks operating in China (foreign and local) would have been one technique. Assuming a reasonable response rate, these results could have met the conventional criteria of statistical generalizability. However, this type of data is not without its difficulties. First, it would not necessarily have provided any substantive detail about the social and historical *context* of firms operating in the sector, or the lived experiences of those working within them. In Chapters 2 and 3, we argued at length that investigating these factors is important for enriching our understanding of management practices in China. Second, the quality of the information gained through survey methods can be somewhat uncertain, especially in the Chinese context. Conducting surveys in state-owned organizations, by definition, requires state permission. Therefore, replies to questionnaires may simply mirror the state-driven policy goals of the organization rather than the complex realities of day-to-day management practices that really interested us. Given our research focus, and our reservations about large-scale surveys, we decided instead to adopt a qualitative research strategy based on a constructivist grounded theory approach.

Constructivist grounded theory

Constructivist grounded theory is a revision of 'classic', or objectivist, grounded theory as developed by Glaser and Strauss (1967). It is a position which fully recognizes that much of the knowledge produced in the social sciences emerges through processes of social construction and interpretation. To quote Charmaz (2016, p. 129), it:

> assumes a relativist epistemology, sees knowledge as socially produced, acknowledges multiple standpoints of both the research participants and the grounded theorist, and takes a reflexive stance towards actions, situations and participants in the field setting – and our [researcher] analytic constructions of them.

As Urquhart (2012) notes, grounded theory is not a unified paradigm and is best characterized as a constantly evolving approach that has been used in different ways at different points in time by researchers of different philosophical orientations. In this study, we used a variety of constructivist grounded theory principles in relation to our data collection and analysis. We justify and elaborate our standpoint on these issues below.

Selecting our methods

As an *interpretive* branch of the social sciences, constructivist grounded theory aims to build a 'thick description' (Geertz, 1973) which may include a variety of sources such as researchers' fieldnotes, participant interviews and relevant documents, including visual material. A fundamental assumption is that methods, *per se*, do not necessarily have to remain tied to a particular philosophical heritage or political standpoint (Urquhart, 2012). As such, a variety of techniques can be used to explore participants' views and feelings as well as the contexts and structures of their lived experience (Charmaz, 2016).

In terms of our own research objectives, there are a number of qualitative methods that might have met our requirements. Ethnographic research, for example, is a technique that offers one of the most significant opportunities to explore the uniqueness and richness of organizational life. However, it is extremely time-consuming and is inevitably limited to the study of a small number of carefully selected organizations. Moreover, given the nature of the businesses we wished to investigate, it would be extremely difficult to access banks for this kind of study. That said, some of the techniques of ethnographic research, such as document analysis, are valuable when studying organizational context. The documents we have used in this study include regulatory and policy documents published by official government bodies, position papers from professional advocacy groups, such as the American and European Chambers of Commerce in China, and media-based event data, such as reports of IPOs, joint ventures and interviews with influential actors. In the interpretivist approach, documents are to be interrogated for their substantive meaning and may act as useful supplements to other sources of data, such as in-depth interviews.

We have chosen in-depth interviews as our key method because they have many advantages that are relevant to our study. To quote Doug Guthrie (1998, p. 219), an experienced researcher of Chinese organizations:

> [W]hile they do not approach the depth of ethnography, the researcher can often learn more about context and thought processes than is possible in a large-scale survey. The researcher can probe, clarify, and ask follow-up questions about a given topic, question, or response. Exploring a subject across a large number of issues allows the researcher to examine ideas of political and institutional structures in a number of different contexts.

As Charmaz (2014) notes, interviewing in a grounded theory study is an *iterative* approach. That is, we begin by selecting participants who have first-hand experience relevant to the research topic and, as soon as the initial round of interviews is completed, data analysis begins. Any unexpected views or actions that emerge in the initial round of interviews are then further investigated through additional interviews based on *theoretical sampling*. In other words, we pursue newly emergent themes in later interviews in an ongoing process of theoretical development. Hence, in this research, we have built a rich, contextually grounded study based on several rounds of interviewing and document analysis, each of which inspired new lines of enquiry.

Assessing 'quality' in constructivist grounded theory

There are a number of perspectives on what kind of 'quality criteria' are relevant when evaluating qualitative research (Rolfe, 2006). At one end of the spectrum are those who argue against using any sort of predetermined criteria because it is not possible to identify a unified 'qualitative paradigm' in the first instance (Sandelowski & Barroso, 2002). Instead, the evaluation of research should be an 'occasion' where readers themselves seek meaning in the report. Thus, judgements are based on a form of reader-response theory (Iser, 1978; Beach, 1993) where the aesthetic quality of the texts, and the rhetorical devices yielded within them, become the focus of evaluation

(Clifford & Marcus, 1986; Geertz, 1988). We have some sympathy with this position but would not go so far as to argue that every individual research item, be it a journal article or a monograph, should be appreciated largely on aesthetic value. We believe our study would be evaluated favourably on these terms, but it is, by definition, up to you, the reader, to make your own judgements about that.

At the other end of the spectrum are those who argue that qualitative research should be assessed using a rather different set of standards than those commonly used in quantitative research. For example, Guba and Lincoln (1998) generated a set of guidelines arguing that 'credibility' in a qualitative study may resemble a form of internal validity, 'dependability' a form of reliability and 'transferability' an equivalent to external validity. Moreover, they argued that qualitative reliability tests could include processes such as 'member checking', which involves participants in the data analysis process and 'peer checking', which means asking colleagues or other experts to check and possibly reanalyze data (Guba & Lincoln, 1998). However, to the extent that we are working within a constructivist tradition, this form of checking somewhat contradicts our underlying assumptions that reality is 'multiple and constructed' and not an essential property of the data. To quote Rolfe (2006, p. 305), 'we should not expect either expert researchers or respondents to arrive at the same themes or categories as the researcher'. Constructivist grounded theory assumes both the relativity of the data and the inevitable subjectivity of data collection and analysis. Nevertheless, the aim is to develop an interpretive understanding that has 'credibility, originality, resonance and usefulness, relative to its historical moment' (Charmaz, 2016, p. 29).

As such, constructivist grounded theorists aim to be as explicit as they can about how their own research position, or standpoint, has influenced the analytic process. One way of doing this is through developing a statement of 'researcher reflexivity' which articulates the researchers' position on a range of relevant issues such as philosophy, methods and theoretical standpoints. In other words, there is an effort to make the research process, in some sense, 'trustworthy' and 'transparent' through being as explicit as possible about the procedures that were used in data collection and data analysis. This is what we have tried to do in this and the following sections of this Methodological Appendix. This introductory section has been a reflexive essay on our research strategy. Section 2 describes our sampling and procedures for the in-depth interviews. Section 3 discusses our document and media-event data analysis. Section 4 provides details on our informants and discusses the ethical implications of the project. Section 5 provides our interview schedule as it developed throughout the research process. In sum, we believe that our research is *credible* because of the strong links we have made between our data and our theoretical analysis; that it is *original* because it is firmly rooted in new empirical insights gleaned from difficult-to-access informants integrated with a comprehensive range of relevant literatures; that it *resonates* in the sophisticated connections it has made between managers' lived experiences and the larger institutional frameworks and power relations in which they are embedded; and that it is *useful* in its challenge to conventional management research assumptions.

Section 2: Sampling, data collection and data analysis procedures for in-depth interviews

Sampling

As we outlined above, grounded theory approaches use an iterative process of data collection based on theoretical sampling. This means that concepts and themes from early interviews are used to guide decisions on where to sample next. Consequently, sampling occurs over several stages. In this project, we began to build our sample by gaining access to managers working in Western banks operating in China. The total population of Western banks in China is, in fact, relatively small. According to the China Financial Services Directory (Guo, 2007), in September 2007, there were 69 banks in total, with 53 from Europe, 13 from North America and three from Australia. The banks selected for our sample were either locally incorporated (offering retail and commercial banking services to Chinese customers), dedicated investment banks or banks with representative offices (which principally provide support to home-based customers doing business in China). Initially 50 bank managers were approached on the basis that their bank was either Tier 1 or Tier 2[1] capitally rated and that they had been established in China for more than 12 months. Of these individuals, ten were previously known to us or had been introduced through a mutual connection. Others were approached through an email or letter explaining the purposes of the project.

Of the 50 that were approached 26 agreed to be interviewed – one from Australia, six from North America and 19 from Europe. Compared to the population, the sample contains a good geographical spread, but has more banks from the Tier 1 range. All the participants were male, and they were aged between 37 and 63. Twenty-three were Caucasian and three were second-generation Chinese-American. The ethnicity of participants is worth commenting on for several reasons. Clearly, foreign banks in China, like other multi-national companies, employ influential local Chinese to grow and conduct their business and it is a common practice for non-Chinese MNCs to employ *xinhauqiao*, overseas Chinese educated in the West (Tung & Worm, 2001). However, the participants initially interviewed, including the Chinese-Americans, can be considered 'outsiders' in that they were nationals of other countries, were not native speakers of Mandarin and had been educated and socialized in a Western context.

As the project progressed, we became interested in exploring participants' understanding of rule interpretation and enforcement in China and the use of power–money networks in the banking sector. We used the snowballing technique (Atkinson & Flint, 2001) to access new informants who might be willing to talk to us about these processes. Consequently, we interviewed a further 14 Western participants in 2009 and 2011. These participants were also male, and they were aged between 33 and 50. Twelve were Caucasian, one was second-generation Chinese-American, and one was second-generation Chinese-Australian. As well as bankers, these individuals also included financial lawyers (two) and ambassadorial officials (two) who were able to offer valuable perspectives, with some analytical distance, on China's legal system and processes of institutional change in the banking sector. Of the ten who were based in banks, seven were from those with Tier 1 rating. In total, 40 Western participants were interviewed.

We also used the snowballing technique to contact local Chinese managers employed by Western banks and interviewed five individuals in 2009. Three of these participants were male and two were female. They were aged between 28 and 36 and were based in Tier 1 banks. We were able to contact a further 14 Chinese nationals through our own connection with an influential Chinese businessman and party official. For reasons of confidentiality, we cannot provide significant details on this contact; however, he was able to help us arrange interviews with managers employed in the state-owned, joint-stock and city-bank sector. These participants were interviewed in 2010 and 2011, and at this point in time we were particularly interested in exploring themes of trust, respect and perceptions of Western banks in the light of the 2008 financial crisis. Twelve were male and two were female and they were between 30 and 57 years old. Thirteen of the participants were fluent English speakers and so their interviews were conducted in English. Seven interviews were conducted in Mandarin by ourselves and an interpreter. The interpreter was a participant we had already interviewed in English and was familiar with the aims of the research project. The interpreter was also known to the Mandarin-speaking participants. In total, 20 Chinese participants, including our principal contact, were interviewed.

While not without its limitations, we believe our sample consists of a heterogeneous group of participants who held a diverse range of views and opinions on the issues that interested us. Further details of our participants are provided in Section 4.

Interviewing procedure

The interviews took place in Hong Kong (12), Shanghai (25), Beijing (18), London (2) and Cambridge, UK (3), between October 2008 and May 2011. The interviews were conducted in a place where the participant felt most comfortable. Some preferred to be interviewed in the workplace, while others preferred more informal settings such as restaurants and coffee bars. The length of interviews varied, with the shortest being approximately 30 minutes and the longest around two hours. On average, interviews were between 45 minutes and one hour. We used an open-ended, in-depth interview format (Charmaz, 2016) which encouraged participants to speak freely about our emergent topics. We used an interview schedule and topic guide to ensure appropriate prompting of relevant topics during the interview. This was developed and modified as the research progressed (see Section 5 for further details).

Extensive notes were taken in each interview and the interviews were recorded in 38 of the 60 interviews. However, 22 participants did not wish to be recorded and the notes taken during these interviews were typed up immediately after the meeting. The interviews conducted in Mandarin were not recorded and the interpreter translated their notes and typed them up shortly after the meetings. The transcriptions of all recorded interviews were checked against recordings. All transcriptions were loaded into ATLAS.ti computer software for data analysis.

Data analysis

As a procedure for data analysis, constructivist grounded theory aims to generate concepts, and the relationships between concepts, which are firmly rooted in the data (Charmaz, 2016; Urquhart, 2012). While breaking down the analytic process into stages is somewhat artificial given the iterative nature of data collection, broadly speaking the stages were as follows. The first stage involved 'initial coding' (or 'open coding' as it was known in the Strauss & Corbin (1998) version of grounded theory). This consisted of tagging repeated words or expressions on a line-by-line basis within each document and encouraged close engagement with the data. Phrases used by participants were sometimes adopted for the coding process, so-called 'in vivo coding'. For example, we used this technique in the section on 'cheating and tricking' in Chapter 8 where we discussed Chinese participants' perceptions of Western bankers.

The second stage involved 'focused coding' where the process of 'constant comparison' began in earnest. Initial codes were compared to identify similarities and differences. This process helps us to understand the relationships *between* concepts as well as their underlying conditions (or structural influences) and their consequences (perceived and actual processes that unfold over time). For example, in Chapter 5, which investigated regulatory reform in the banking sector, we identified a variety of narratives on the utility of those changes. The ways in which the American Chamber of Commerce constructed a narrative on the value of 'free market competition' betrayed their belief in the universal applicability of rational choice economics and their view of the consequences, for China, of 'deviating' from this approach. Analyzing the data from a constructivist standpoint means paying close attention to the language used by participants and the authors of documents so as to identify the 'taken for granted' properties of the terms they use. By studying these *how* processes we were able to conceptualize *why* they reacted in the way they did by situating their narratives within broader explanatory concepts such as power relations and historical memory. It was possible to divide the participants into groups based on emerging codes and concepts;

hence numbers are provided for these in Chapters 5 to 8. However, these should not be taken as an indicator of statistical generalizability but, rather, an indication of convergent or divergent views in our particular sample on the theme under investigation.

The third stage of analysis used theoretical codes to 'weave the fractured story back together' (Glaser, 1978, p. 72). In the early writings on grounded theory, there was an assumption that the researcher should attempt to leave behind their knowledge of the existing theoretical debates and develop a novel theory entirely based on the data (Glaser & Strauss, 1967; Glaser, 1978). However, there is now an acknowledgement that it is not possible to dismiss our existing knowledge and the aim is to develop an 'informed grounded theory' (Thornberg, 2012) such that a study is rooted in the data by grounded theory methods while, simultaneously, being informed by relevant literature and theoretical concepts. When building a constructivist grounded theory, there is a place for adopting explanatory concepts from a variety of disciplinary fields, where they are relevant to a particular data set. In this study, theoretical codes based on concepts such as 'power relations' and 'historical memory' have helped us to interpret the data and build an overarching explanatory account which spans the study as a whole.

We also used 'memos' to build our codes back into a narrative form. Writing memos throughout the project helped us to define *why* some concepts were important, *what* the properties were of emergent categories, *how* a category arose in the first instance, *which* particular consequences were associated with the concept, and so on. Memos were useful aids in the writing-up phase of the research where we began to construct our own narrative and interpretation of the principal 'stories' of our participants. There are several ways of presenting the findings in constructivist grounded theories, with some preferring to use diagrams or matrices to present data. In this monograph, we were lucky enough to have the space to present the full context of the study and to provide a rich chain of evidence nested within a robust theoretical framework. We chose to present this in a narrative form which is now widely adopted in constructivist grounded theory approach (Charmaz, 2016). It is our 'story', but it is firmly located in our data.

Section 3: Documents and media-based event data

This study utilized documents produced the China Banking Regulatory Commission (CBRC), the American Chamber of Commerce in China (ACCC) and the European Union Chamber of Commerce in China (EUCCC). We also drew on media-based event data, such as coverage of relevant IPOs, joint ventures and opinion pieces by key figures in the Chinese and Western banking sectors. The documents were integrated with our interviews and we used the same processes of data analysis and theory development as described in Section 2. In this section, we highlight some important research issues which accompany the use of documents in social research.

Documents

Documents need to be understood in relation to the context in which they were produced. To quote Atkinson and Coffey (2004, p. 58), they are not simply 'transparent representations' of a given organization. Rather, they need to be read with a sensitivity to the goals they are trying to accomplish and with an awareness of their 'implied readership'. The documents we have used in this study were certainly written to make an impression. The documents published by the CBRC were available in Mandarin and English, and we were aware that both versions were written with an international readership in mind. The various procedures described within them were published in an effort to increase the credibility of the CBRC in a global financial arena. While the CBRC is technically an independent body in Chinese law (Cousin, 2011), it remains heavily influenced by the state and any published documents need to be understood with this in mind. Likewise, the documents published by the ACCC and the EUCCC had partly been written to make an impression on Chinese policy-makers. The documents identified problems in the business environment in China, as identified by members of the Chambers. We focused mainly on documents published by the Banking and Finance groups but were aware that these were essentially advocacy documents arguing the case for a particular interest group.

We did not simply interpret documents at face value. Documents are interesting precisely because they may present the opinions and prejudices of policy-makers and members of the business community. Thus, while documents indicated the intentions of policies and the concerns of professional associations, our interviews disclosed a variety of perceptions on how policies are actually implemented and experienced within an organization.

Media-based event data

Media-based event data are drawn from a range of print and electronic sources including newspapers, television and web-based articles. As with other documents, these data are not to be taken at face value. There are two generally recognized sources of potential bias in media-based event data (Earl et al., 2004). The first is *selection bias*, which in this arena means that commercial and political factors influence the events that media organizations choose to cover. In this study, for example, we would acknowledge that some of the events we selected, such as the stories on social networking and company malpractice, may well be under-reported, or only sensationally reported in relation to events that occur in a non-Western setting (Cook et al., 2017).

The second issue is *description bias* which relates to the accuracy of the media coverage of any given event (Ortiz et al., 2005). In the main, media reports may offer an accurate account of the 'hard facts' about an event (Earl et al., 2004). That is, they are usually correct about the 'who', 'what', 'when' and 'where' of events and any errors can be checked through cross-referral to other reports. For example, in this study, using media-based event data, we can be certain that the ABC (who) held an IPO (what) in April 2010 (when) in Hong Kong and Shanghai (where). Soft news, on the other hand, refers to the 'impressions and inferences of journalists and commentators' (Earl et al., 2004, p. 19) and may be prone to misrepresentation or framing events in a negative light (e.g. the tendency in British media to portray industrial action in a negative way).

While these impressions may be described as a potential source of 'bias' (Ortiz et al., 2005), in our study it is precisely these subjective interpretations which are of interest to us as social scientists. In this study we used media-based event data to incorporate the voices of a range of political actors (see, for example, the interviews with Li Kaisheng, Chairman of the China Banking Regulator Commission reported in Chapter 5, and an interview with Li Wei, Deputy Chair of the SASAC, reported in Chapter 8). We did not attempt to analyze these interviews as 'fact'. Rather, we sought to contextualize them in relation to how they justified certain actions of the Chinese regulators and made various judgements on the behaviours of Western banks. In other words, as with other documents, we treated them as *representations* and integrated them into our analyses accordingly.

Section 4: Dealing with sensitive topics, ethical considerations and details of informants

Sensitive topics

Some of the themes we investigated, such as *guanxi* and *guanxi* practice, are considered rather sensitive research topics because, in some circumstances, they may be associated with unethical or illegal conduct (Guthrie, 1998). As such, managers may deny any knowledge of the topic or lie about their actions in relation to the concept. However, it is now generally established that gleaning information on sensitive topics can often be accomplished through in-depth interviewing, particularly when the topic can be nested with more general questions. This was the strategy we adopted in this study. There are, of course, always difficult methodological issues when investigating sensitive topics, and the data presented here needs to be understood as contingent and incomplete. But the fact that some managers *were* prepared to talk openly about a range of sensitive topics, such as murky loan applications, questionable *guanxi* networks and low opinions of their joint venture partners, opened a whole new side of organizational life to our investigation. Our participants expressed a wide range of views on a range of topics which indicates that our techniques had sufficient validity to address our research objectives.

Ethical considerations

Interviews were conducted under conditions of anonymity and confidentiality. It is not possible to reveal the identity of the banks because, given the seniority of some of the individuals interviewed, this could lead to the identification of the participant. Similarly, we are unable to provide very specific details about informants as this could potentially breach the interview condition of anonymity.

We owe a lot to our participants who were surprisingly open when answering our questions and gave generously of their time and energy. Nothing was offered in exchange for their participation, but we have maintained and developed friendships with some of them and continue to enjoy their company and hospitality in China and elsewhere.

Details of informants

Below is a list providing further details on our participants. These indicate, in general terms, their position, their place of origin, where they were interviewed and the date of their interview. Each number indicates one interview and corresponds to the relevant quotation in the text.

1 Commercial Banking Manager, Western, Beijing, 2008
2 Relationship Manager, Western, Beijing, 2008
3 Head of Wealth Management, Western, Beijing, 2008
4 General Manager, Western, Hong Kong, 2008
5 Chief Executive Officer, Western, Hong Kong, 2008
6 Regional CEO, Western, Hong Kong, 2008
7 Expatriate Government Official, Western, London, 2009
8 Chief Representative Officer, Western, Hong Kong, 2009
9 HR Operations Manager, Western, Hong Kong, 2009
10 Regional CEO, Western, Hong Kong, 2009
11 IT Development Manager, Chinese, Hong Kong, 2009
12 Expatriate Lawyer, Western, Hong Kong, 2009
13 Management Consultant, Western, Cambridge, 2009
14 Expatriate Lawyer, Western, Shanghai, 2009
15 Management Consultant, Western, Shanghai, 2009
16 Business HR Manager, Chinese, Shanghai, 2009
17 Expatriate Government Official, Western, Hong Kong, 2009
18 Regional Chief Operating Officer, Western, Hong Kong, 2009
19 General Manager, Chinese, Hong Kong, 2009
20 Chief Financial Officer, Western, Hong Kong, 2009
21 General Manager, Chinese, Shanghai, 2009
22 Chief Operating Officer, Western, Shanghai, 2009
23 Regional CEO, Western, Shanghai, 2009
24 Head of Retail Lending Products, Western, Shanghai, 2009
25 Chief Executive Officer, Chinese, Shanghai, 2009
26 Regional CEO, Western, Shanghai, 2009
27 IT Director, Western, Shanghai, 2010
28 Credit Review Manager, Western, Shanghai, 2010

29 JV Director, Western, Shanghai, 2010
30 Business HR Manager, Western, Shanghai, 2010
31 Brand and Marketing Manager, Western, Shanghai, 2010
32 Representative Officer, Western, Shanghai, 2010
33 Regional CEO, Western, Shanghai, 2010
34 Vice President, Western, Shanghai, 2010
35 Retail Product Development Manager, Western, Beijing, 2010
36 Vice President, Chinese, Beijing, 2010
37 Credit Review Manager, Chinese, Beijing, 2010
38 Executive Director, Western, Beijing, 2010
39 Retail Banking Manager, Western, Beijing, 2010
40 General Manager, Western, Beijing, 2010
41 Senior Relationship Manager, Western, Beijing, 2010
42 General Manager, Chinese, Beijing, 2010
43 General Manager, Chinese, Beijing, 2010
44 Brand & Marketing Manager, Chinese, Beijing, 2010
45 Investment Banker, Chinese, Beijing, 2010
46 Management Consultant, Chinese, Beijing, 2010
47 Investment Banker, Western, Cambridge, 2011
48 Vice President, Western, Cambridge, 2011
49 Head of Retail Banking, Western, London, 2011
50 General Manager, Western, Beijing, 2011
51 Head of Wealth Management, Chinese, Beijing, 2011
52 Business HR Manager, Chinese, Shanghai, 2011
53 Director of Wealth Management, Chinese, Shanghai, 2011
54 Chief Operating Officer, Western, Shanghai, 2011
55 Chief Financial Officer, Chinese, Shanghai, 2011
56 Investment Banker, Chinese, Shanghai, 2011
57 Senior Relationship Manager, Chinese, Shanghai, 2011
58 General Manager, Western, Shanghai, 2011
59 Chief Operating Officer, Chinese, Shanghai, 2011
60 General Manager, Chinese, Shanghai, 2011

Section 5: Interview schedule

In the in-depth interviews, questions were open-ended but were based around four main categories related to our research questions: (i) perceptions of state-level regulations and how they operate at the organizational level; (ii) perceptions of changes in corporate governance in Chinese banks and the role of Western banks and investors in that process; (iii) perceptions on the importance of networking in relation to establishing businesses in China; and (iv) perceptions of the nature of trust relationships between the two groups and views on how those had been influenced by the banking crisis.

Our technique means that questions are not necessarily conducted in the same sequential order or using the exact same wording. Rather, a 'conversational approach' was adopted to help the participant feel at ease (Charmaz, 2016). We did, however, aim to cover all topics in the schedule with each participant where this was practical. If a participant began to close on a particular topic, probing and encouragement was used to try to elicit a response. However, this was not pursued if it was clear the participant did not wish to discuss a particular issue.

Interview schedule

ORGANIZATION (name) ________________________________
RESPONDENT
(name, position, age) ________________________________
Date of interview ________________________________
Interview length ________________________________

WARM-UP QUESTIONS

1 Can you tell me how long you've worked for (organization)?
2 Can you tell me about your current responsibilities and duties?
3 What have been your biggest achievements so far?
4 What have been your most challenging experiences?

REGULATORY ENVIRONMENT QUESTION

1 What kinds of banking regulations are important for your organization?
2 What has been your experience of the implementation of new regulations?
3 Do you think regulations are clearly communicated by the regulator to your bank?
4 What do you think might be the source of difficulties in developing banking regulations in China?
5 What do you think might be the source of difficulties in enforcing the regulations?

CORPORATE GOVERNANCE QUESTIONS

1 How do you think Western banks contribute to corporate governance issues in China?
2 Why do you think Chinese banks have wanted to work with Western banks to improve corporate governance?
3 What have been the key improvements made to corporate governance by collaborations between Western and Chinese banks?
4 What challenges have Western banks faced in this process?
5 What challenges do you think Chinese banks face in implementing corporate governance reforms?

SOCIAL NETWORKING QUESTIONS

1 How important do you think *guanxi* networks are when working in China?
2 How would you define a *guanxi* network? Is it the same as other forms of network in other parts of the world?
3 What kind of things do you do to build your guanxi networks?

TRUST RELATIONSHIP QUESTIONS

1 How well do you get on with your Western/Chinese partners?
2 What kinds of things make it easy to build good relationships with your partners?
3 What sorts of things happen in the workplace that make building good relationships difficult?
4 What could your partner do to improve your relationship?
5 Have external factors, like the banking crisis, changed your relationships with your partner? Why might that be?

CLOSING

1 Do you have any suggestions for other topics we could consider in this research project?
2 Thank participant and reiterate terms of confidentiality and anonymity.

Note

1 Tier rating indicates the size of capital adequacy in the bank as assessed by regulators. Tier 1 represents a bank with more resources than a Tier 2 institution.

References

ACCC (2009b). *White paper part 2: Industry issues.* Beijing: American Chamber of Commerce in China. Retrieved from: www.amchamchina.org/policy-advocacy/whitepaper.

Adler, N. J. & Boyacigiller, N. (1996). 'Global management and the 21st century'. In B. J. Punnet & O. Shenkar (Eds), *Handbook for international management research* (pp. 537–558). Cambridge, MA: Blackwell Business.

Aguilera, R. V. & Jackson, G. (2003). 'The cross-national diversity of corporate governance: Dimensions and determinants'. *Academy of Management Review*, 28(3), 447–465.

Alexander, P. (2013, July 1). 'Top 1000 World Banks'. *The Banker*. Retrieved from: www.thebanker.com/Banker-Data/Banker-Rankings/Top-1000-World-Banks-2013?ct=true.

Altenburg, T., Schmitz, H. & Stamm, A. (2008). 'Breakthrough? China's and India's transition from production to innovation'. *World Development*, 36(2), 325–344.

American Chamber of Commerce in China (ACCC) (2009a). *White paper part 1: The business climate for American firms in China*. Beijing: American Chamber of Commerce in China. Retrieved from: www.amchamchina.org/policy-advocacy/white-paper.

Atkinson, P. & Coffey, A. (2004). 'Analysing documentary realities'. In D. Silverman (Ed.), *Qualitative research* (pp. 77–93). London: Sage.

Atkinson, R. & Flint, J. (2001). 'Accessing hidden and hard-to-reach populations: Snowball research strategies'. *Social Research Update*, 33(1), 1–4.

Bachman, D. (2006). *Bureaucracy, economy, and leadership in China: The institutional origins of the Great Leap Forward*. Cambridge: Cambridge University Press.

Bachrach, P. & Baratz, M. S. (1962). 'Two faces of power'. *American Political Science Review*, 56(4), 947–952.

Baker, A. (2010). 'Restraining regulatory capture? Anglo-America, crisis politics andtrajectories of change in global financial governance'. *International Affairs*, 86(3), 647–663.

Barbalet, J. (2017). 'Guanxi as social exchange: Emotions, power and corruption'. *Sociology*, Retrieved from: https://doi.org/10.1177/0038038517692511.

Barreto, E. & Rudegeair, P. (2013, September 4). 'BofA exits stake in China's CCB with $1.5 billion sale'. Reuters. Retrieved from: www.reuters.com/article/us-bankofamerica-china/bofa-exits-stake-in-chinas-ccb-with-1-5-billion-sale-idUSBRE98209P20130904.

Barthes, R. (1972). *Mythologies.* London: Vintage.

Basel Committee (2010). 'Basel III: A global regulatory framework for more resilient banks and banking systems'. *Basel Committee on Banking Supervision*. Basel: Basel Committee.

Bauer, P. W., Berger, A. N., Ferrier, G. D. & Humphrey, D. B. (1998). 'Consistency conditions for regulatory analysis of financial institutions: A comparison of frontier efficiency methods'. *Journal of Economics and Business*, 50(2), 85–114.

Beach, R. (1993). *A teacher's introduction to reader-response theories*. Urbana, IL: National Council of Teachers of English.

Bell, S. & Feng, H. (2013). *The rise of the People's Bank of China*. Cambridge, MA: Harvard University Press.

Berg, M. (2006). 'Britain, industry and perceptions of China: Matthew Boulton, 'useful knowledge' and the Macartney Embassy to China 1792–1794'. *Journal of Global History*, 1(2), 269–288.

Berger, P. & Luckmann, T. (1966). *The social construction of reality*. London: Penguin.

Bian, Y. (2018). 'The prevalence and increasing significance of guanxi'. *China Quarterly* (forthcoming).

Bickers, R. (2017). *Out of China: How the Chinese ended the era of Western domination*. London: Allen Lane.

Blair, M. (1996). *Ownership and control: Rethinking corporate governance for the twenty-first century*. Washington, DC: The Brookings Institution.

Bo, W. (2010, July 8). 'ABC's IPO reflects changing banking paradigm'. *China Daily*. Retrieved from: www.chinadaily.com.cn/business/2010-07/08/content_10081778.htm

Boisot, M. & Child, J. (1996). 'From fiefs to clans and network capitalism: Explaining China's emerging economic order'. *Administrative Science Quarterly*, 41(4), 600–628.

Bourdieu, P. (1984). *Distinction: A social critique of the judgement of taste*. Cambridge, MA: Harvard University Press.

Bourdieu, P. (1986). 'The forms of capital'. In: J. Richardson (Ed.), *Handbook of theory and research for the sociology of education* (pp. 241–258). New York: Greenwood.

Bourdieu, P. (2005). *The social structures of the economy*. Cambridge: Polity.

Bowles, P. & White, G. (1993). *The political economy of China's financial reforms*. Oxford: Westview Press.

Boyacigiller, N. A. & Adler, N. J. (1991). 'The parochial dinosaur: Organizational science in a global context'. *Academy of Management Review*, 16(2), 262–290.

Bracking, S. (2009). *Money and power: Great predators in the political economy of development*. London: Pluto Press.

Brahm, L. (2002). *Zhu Rongji and the transformation of modern China*. Singapore: John Wiley & Sons.

Brehm, S. (2008). 'Risk management in China's state banks: International best practice and the political economy of regulation'. *Business and Politics*, 10(1), 1–29.

Brødsgaard, K. E. (2012). 'Politics and business group formation in China: The party in control?' *The China Quarterly*, 211, 624–648.

Buck, T., Filatotchev, I., Nolan, P. H. & Wright, M. (2001). 'Different paths to economic reform in Russia and China: Causes and consequences'. *Journal of World Business*, 35(4), 379–400.

Buckley, P. J., Clegg, L. J., Voss, H., Cross, A. R., Liu, X. & Zheng, P. (2018). 'A retrospective and agenda for future research on Chinese outward foreign direct investment'. *Journal of International Business Studies*, 1–20.

Callahan, W. A. (2012). 'Sino-speak: Chinese exceptionalism and the politics of history'. *The Journal of Asian Studies*, 71(1), 33–55.

Callahan, W. A. (2014). 'Chinese exceptionalism and the politics of history'. In N. Horesh & E. Kavalski (Eds), *Asian thought on China's changing international relations* (pp. 17–33). Basingstoke: Palgrave Macmillan.

Campbell, J. (2004). *Institutional change and globalization*. Princetown, NJ: Princetown University Press.

Campbell, T. L. & Keys, P. Y. (2002). 'Corporate governance in South Korea: The chaebol experience'. *Journal of Corporate Finance*, 8(4), 373–391.

Cassin, R. (2016, February 24). 'HSBC: SEC investigating Asia hiring practices'. The FCPA Blog. Retrieved from www.fcpablog.com/blog/2016/2/24/hsbc-sec-investigating-asia-hiring-practices.html.

CBRC (2003). *Annual Report 2002*. Beijing: CBRC.

CBRC (2005). *Latest developments in China's banking reform, opening-up and supervison*. Beijing: CBRC. Retrieved from: www.cbrc.gov.cn/chinese/home/docView/1764.html.

CBRC (2006). *Annual Report 2005*. Beijing: CBRC.

CBRC (2012). *Annual Report 2011*. Beijing: CBRC.

CBRC (2014) *Annual Report 2013*. Beijing: CBRC. Retrieved from: www.cbrc.gov.cn/chinese/files/2014/A2726BEBE1AA406BB5CAC4ADA3875D35.pdf.

CBRC (2016). *Annual Report 2015*. Beijing: CBRC. Retrieved from: www.cbrc.gov.cn/chinese/files/2016/6C1DEC063D6442B289B7C24F662D2E52.pdf.

'CBRC moves to regulate derivatives' (2009, July 8). *Global Times*. Retrieved from: www.globaltimes.cn/content/455458.shtml.

Chang, K. C. (2011). 'A path to understanding guanxi in China's transitional economy: Variations on network behavior'. *Sociological Theory*, 29(4), 315–339.

Charmaz, K. (2014). *Constructing grounded theory*. London: Sage.

Charmaz, K. (2016). 'Constructivist grounded theory methods'. In J. M. Morse, P. N. Stern, J. Corbin, B. Bowers, K. Charmaz & A. E. Clarke (Eds), *Developing grounded theory: The second generation* (pp. 127–154). London: Routledge.

Chen, C. C., Chen, X. P. & Huang, S. (2013). 'Chinese Guanxi: An integrative review and new directions for future research. 中国人的关系: 综合文献回顾及未来研究方向'. *Management and Organization Review*, 9(1), 167–207.

Chen, G. & Eder, S. (2009, November 10). 'A Morgan Stanley star falls in China'. Reuters. Retrieved from www.reuters.com/article/us-china-corruption/a-morgan-stanley-star-falls-in-china-idUSTRE5A94AY20091110.

Cheng, L. (2003). *Banking in modern China: Entrepreneurs, professional managers, and the development of Chinese banks, 1897–1937*. Cambridge: Cambridge University Press.

Child, J. (2000). 'Theorizing about organization cross-nationally'. In J. Cheng & R. Peterson (Eds), *Advances in international comparative management* (pp. 27–76). Stamford: JAI Press.

Child, J. (2009). 'Context, comparison, and methodology in Chinese management research'. *Management and Organization Review*, 5(1), 57–73.

Child, J. & Lu, Y. (1990). 'Industrial decision-making under China's reform, 1985–1988'. *Organization Studies*, 11(3), 321–351.

China Banking Regulatory Commission (CBRC) (2003a). The China banking regulatory commission will hold the first conference of the Council of International Advisers. Press Release. Retrieved from: www.cbrc.gov.cn/EngdocView.do?docID=484

China Statistical Yearbook. (2014). Beijing: Chinese Statistical Bureau.

China UnionPay. (2016). Overview. Retrieved from: http://en.unionpay.com/comInstr/aboutUs/file_4912292.html.

'China wall hit by global bank with 2% share' (2012, June 5). *Bloomberg*. Retrieved from: www.bloomberg.com/news/articles/2012-06-04/china-wall-hit-by-global-banks-with-2-market-share.

'Chinese official raps foreign banks on derivatives'. (2009, December 4). The Associated Press. Retrieved from: www.newsday.com/business/chinese-official-raps-foreign-banks-on-derivatives-1.1637008.

Chwieroth, J. M. (2007). 'Neoliberal economists and capital account liberalization in emerging markets'. *International Organization*, 61(2), 443–463.

Claessens, S. & Horen, N. (2014). 'Foreign banks: Trends and impact'. *Journal of Money, Credit and Banking*, 46(1), 295–326.

Clarke, D. C. (2003). 'Corporate governance in China: An overview'. *China Economic Review*, 14, 494–507.

Clarke, D. C. (2011). '"Nothing but wind"? The past and future of comparative corporate governance'. *The American Journal of Comparative Law*, 59(1), 75–110.

Clegg, S. (2010). 'The state, power, and agency: Missing in action in institutional theory?' *Journal of Management Inquiry*, 19(1), 4–13.

Clegg, S. R. (1989). *Frameworks of power*. London: Sage.

Clifford, J. & Marcus, G. E. (Eds). (1986). *Writing culture: The poetics and politics of ethnography*. Berkeley: University of California Press.

Coble, P. M. (1986). *The Shanghai capitalists and the Nationalist government, 1927–1937*. Cambridge, MA: Harvard East Asian Monographs.

Coffee, J. C. (2009). 'What went wrong? An initial inquiry into the causes of the 2008 financial crisis'. *Journal of Corporate Law Studies*, 9(1), 1–22.

Cook, S. J., Blas, B., Carroll, R. J. & Sinha, S. (2017). 'Two wrongs make a right: Addressing underreporting in binary data from multiple sources'. *Political Analysis*, 25(2), 223–240.

Corsetti, G., Pesenti, P. & Roubini, N. (1999). 'What caused the Asian currency and financial crisis?' *Japan and the World Economy*, 11(3), 305–373.

Cousin, V. (2007). *Banking in China*. Basingstoke: Palgrave Macmillan.

Cousin, V. (2011). *Banking in China* (2nd edition). Basingstoke: Palgrave Macmillan.

Dahl, R. A. (1957). 'The concept of power'. *Behavioral Science*, 2(3), 201–215.

Das, T. K. & Teng, B. S. (1998). 'Between trust and control: Developing confidence in partner cooperation in alliances'. *Academy of Management Review*, 23(3), 491–512.

DiMaggio, P. & Powell, W. (1983). 'The iron cage revisited: Institutional isomorphism and collective rationality in organizational fields'. *American Sociological Review*, 48(2), 147–160.

Dye, J. (2012, August 16). 'Ex-Morgan Stanley executive gets prison time in bribery case'. Reuters. Retrieved from www.reuters.com/article/us-morganstanley-bribery-sentencing/ex-morgan-stanley-executive-gets-prison-time-in-bribery-case-idUSBR E87F1DV20120816

Earl, J., Martin, A., McCarthy, J. D. & Soule, S. A. (2004). 'The use of newspaper data in the study of collective action'. *Annual Review of Sociology*, 30, 65–80.

Earley, P. C. (2006). 'Leading cultural research in the future: A matter of paradigms and taste'. *Journal of International Business Studies*, 37(6), 922–931.

Edwards, V., Polonsky, G., Pucko, D., Warner, M. & Zhu, Y. (2005). *Management in transitional economies: From the Berlin Wall to the Great Wall of China*. London: Routledge.

Elias, N. & Jephcott, E. (1978). *The civilizing process.* Oxford: Blackwell.

Ermisch, J. & Gambetta, D. (2010). 'Do strong family ties inhibit trust?' *Journal of Economic Behavior and Organization*, 75(3), 365–376.

European Chamber of Commerce in China (EUCCC) (2008). *European business in China position paper: Executive summary.* Beijing: European Chambers of Commerce in China.

EUCCC (2009). *European Chamber business confidence survey 2009.* Beijing: European Chambers of Commerce in China. Retrieved from www.europeanchamber.com.cn/en/european-chamber-publications.

EUCCC (2010a). *European Chamber business confidence survey 2010.* Beijing: European Chambers of Commerce in China. Retrieved from www.europeanchamber.com.cn/en/european-chamber-publications.

EUCCC (2010b). *European business in China position paper 2009/2010: Executive summary.* Beijing: European Chambers of Commerce in China. Retrieved from: www.europeanchamber.com.cn/en/european-chamber-publications.

EUCCC (2010c). *European business in China position paper 2009/2010: Banking and securities working group.* Beijing: European Chambers of Commerce in China. Retrieved from: www.europeanchamber.com.cn/en/european-chamber-publications.

'Eyes on the home front' (2009, November 30). *China Economic Review.* Retrieved from: https://chinaeconomicreview.com/eyes-on-the-home-front.

Fairbank, J., Feuerwerker, A. & Twitchett, D. (Eds). (1986). *The Cambridge history of China, Vol 11, Late Ch'ing 1800–1911.* Cambridge: Cambridge University Press.

Ferri, G. (2009). 'Are new tigers supplanting old mammoths in China's banking system? Evidence from a sample of city commercial banks'. *Journal of Banking & Finance*, 33(1), 131–140.

Fligstein, N. (2002). *The architecture of markets: An economic sociology of twenty-first-century capitalist societies.* Princeton: Princeton University Press.

Fligstein, N. & McAdam, D. (2012). *A theory of fields.* Oxford: Oxford University Press.

Foucault, M. (1977). *Discipline and punish: The birth of the prison.* New York: Vintage.

Foucault, M. (1980). *Power/knowledge: Selected interviews and other writings, 1972–1977.* New York: Pantheon.

Freeman, C. W. & Yuan, W. J. (2011). *China's New Leftists and the China model debate after the financial crisis.* Washington, DC: Center for Strategic and International Studies.

Freeman, C. W. & Yuan, W. J. (2012). 'The Influence and Illusion of China's New Left'. *The Washington Quarterly*, 35(1), 65–82.

Fukuyama, F. (1995). *Trust: The social virtues and the creation of prosperity.* New York: Free press.

G-20 Communique (2009, April 2). *London summit leaders' statement.* Retrieved from: www.imf.org/external/np/sec/pr/2009/pdf/g20_040209.pdf

Gad, C. & Jensen, C. B. (2014). 'The promises of practice'. *The Sociological Review*, 62(4), 698–718.

Galbraith, A. & Zhou, W. (2017, June 20). 'Protectionism hurts China's financial sector, opening helps: PBOC's Zhou'. Reuters. Retrieved from: www.reuters.com/article/us-china-economy-finance/protectionism-hurts-chinas-financial-sector-opening-helps-pbocs-zhou-idUSKBN19B04P.

Gane, M. (Ed.). (2013). *Towards a critique of Foucault: Foucault, Lacan and the question of ethics.* London: Routledge.

Gao, H. M. (2007, November 17). 'Chinese companies going global: Operational strategies and communication challenges'. *China Currents.* Retrieved from: www.china center.net/chinese-companies-going-global-operational-strategies-and-communication-challenges.

García-Herrero, A., Gavilá, S. & Santabárbara, D. (2006). 'China's banking reform: An assessment of its evolution and possible impact'. *CESifo Economic Studies,* 52(2), 304–363.

Garnaut, J. (2010, October 2). 'The Princelings'. *The Sydney Morning Herald.* Retrieved from: www.smh.com.au/business/the-princelings-20101001-1613l.html.

Geertz, C. (1973). *The interpretation of cultures: Selected essays.* New York: Basic Books.

Geertz, C. (1988). *Works and lives: The anthropologist as author.* Stanford, CA: Stanford University Press.

Gewirtz, J. (2017). *Unlikely partners: Chinese reformers, Western economists and the making of global China.* Cambridge, MA: Harvard University Press.

Giddens, A. (1984). *The constitution of society: Outline of the theory of structuration.* Berkeley: University of California Press.

Glaser, B. G. (1978). *Theoretical sensitivity: Advances in the methodology of grounded theory.* Mill Valley, CA: Sociology Press.

Glaser, B. & Strauss, A. (1967). *The discovery of grounded theory.* New Brunswick: Transaction Publishers.

Gold, T., Guthrie, D. & Wank, D. (Eds). (2002). *Social connections in China: Institutions, culture, and the changing nature of guanxi.* Cambridge: Cambridge University Press.

'Goldman Sachs: A history of controversy'. (2010, April 19). *The Telegraph.* Retrieved from: www.telegraph.co.uk/finance/newsbysector/banksandfinance/7608325/Goldma n-Sachs-a-history-of-controversy.html.

Granovetter, M. (1985). 'Economic action and social structure: The problem of embeddedness'. *American Journal of Sociology,* 481–510.

Gu, F. & Nolan, J. (2017). 'Performance appraisal in Western and local banks in China: The influence of firm ownership on the perceived importance of guanxi'. *The International Journal of Human Resource Management,* 28(10), 1433–1453.

Guba, E. G. & Lincoln Y. S. (1998). 'Competing paradigms in qualitative research'. In N. Denzin & Y. Lincoln (Eds), *The Landscape of qualitative research: Theory and issues* (pp. 195–222). Thousand Oaks, CA: Sage.

Guo, A. (Ed.). (2007). *China financial service directory.* Hong Kong: Economic Review Publishing.

Guo, S. (2006). *The political economy of Asian transition from communism.* Aldershot: Ashgate.

Guthrie, D. (1998). 'The declining significance of guanxi in China's economic transition'. *The China Quarterly,* 154(June), 254–282.

Guthrie, D. (2001). *Dragon in a three-piece suit: The emergence of capitalism in China.* Princeton: Princeton University Press.

Hafer, R. W. (2005). *The federal reserve system: An encyclopedia.* Westport: Greenwood Press.

Hall, P. A. & Taylor, R. C. (1996). 'Political science and the three new institutionalisms'. *Political Studies,* 44(5), 936–957.

Hamid, J. & Tenev, S. (2008). 'Transforming China's banks: The IFC's experience'. *Journal of Contemporary China,* 17(5), 449–468.

Hamilton, G. G. (1990). 'Patriarchy, patrimonialism, and filial piety: A comparison of China and Western Europe'. *British Journal of Sociology*, 41(1), 77–104.

Hamilton, G. G. (2006). *Commerce and capitalism in Chinese societies*. London: Routledge.

Hampden-Turner, C. & Trompenaars, A. (1993). *The seven cultures of capitalism: Value systems for creating wealth in the United States, Japan, Germany, France, Britain, Sweden, and the Netherlands*. New York: Doubleday.

Harbison, F. H. & Myers, C. A. (1959). *Management in the industrial world: An international analysis*. New York: McGraw-Hill.

Harris, J. (2012). 'Outward bound: transnational capitalism in China'. *Race & Class*, 54(1), 13–32.

Hawes, C. & Chiu, T. (2007). 'Foreign strategic investors in the Chinese banking market: Cultural shift or business as usual?' *Banking & Finance Law Review*, 22(2), 203–237.

He, W. & Ping, H. W. (2014). *Banking regulation in China: The role of public and private sectors*. Berlin: Springer.

Hevia, J. L. (1995). *Cherishing men from afar: Qing guest ritual and the Macartney Embassy of 1793*. Durham, NC: Duke University Press.

Ho, H. (2006, April 7). 'CBRC concerned about selling Chinese banks'. Risk.net. Retrieved from: www.risk.net/derivatives/structured-products/1505894/cbrc-concerned-about-selling-chinese-banks.

Hofstede, G. (1984). *Culture's consequences: International differences in work-related values*. London: Sage.

Hofstede, G. H. (2001). *Culture's consequences: Comparing values, behaviors, institutions and organizations across nations*. London: Sage.

Hofstede, G. (2006). 'What did GLOBE really measure? Researchers' minds versus respondents' minds'. *Journal of International Business Studies*, 37(6), 882–896.

Hofstede, G. (2011). 'Dimensionalizing Cultures: The Hofstede Model in Context'. *Online Readings in Psychology and Culture*, 2(1).

Hofstede, G. & Bond, M. H. (1988). 'The Confucius connection: From cultural roots to economic growth'. *Organizational Dynamics*, 16(4), 5–21.

Horner, C. (2009). *Rising China and its postmodern fate: Memories of empire in a new global context*. Athens, GA: University of Georgia Press.

House, R. J., Hanges, P. J., Javidan, M., Dorfman, P. W. & Gupta, V. (Eds). (2004). *Culture, leadership, and organizations: The GLOBE study of 62 societies*. London: Sage.

Huff, L. & Kelley, L. (2003). 'Levels of organizational trust in individualist versus collectivist societies: A seven-nation study'. *Organization Science*, 14(1), 81–90.

Huiyin, C. (2008, October 31). 'Citic Pacific stung by "cowboy" investment'. *Caijing*. Retrieved from: http://english.caijing.com.cn/2008-10-31/110025046.html

Institute of International Finance (IIF) (2006). *Corporate governance in China: An investor perspective*. Washington, DC: IIF Task Force Report.

International Finance Corporation (IFC) (2012, November). *IFC's Role in China's Financial Sector Transformation*. Washington, DC: IFC Impact Report.

Iser, W. (1978). *The act of reading: A theory of aesthetic response*. Baltimore, MD: Johns Hopkins University Press.

Jack, G. & Westwood, R. (2009). *International and cross-cultural management studies: A postcolonial reading*. London: Palgrave Macmillan.

Jacob, R. & Rabinovitch, S. (2011, October 18) 'China SMEs rely on shadow financing for growth'. *Financial Times*. Retrieved from: www.ft.com/content/31180230-f97b-11e0-bf8f-00144feab49a.

Jacques, M. (2009). *When China rules the world: The rise of the middle kingdom and the end of the Western world*. London: Penguin.

Javidan, M., House, R. J., Dorfman, P. W., Hanges, P. J. & De Luque, M. S. (2006). 'Conceptualizing and measuring cultures and their consequences: A comparative review of GLOBE's and Hofstede's approaches'. *Journal of International Business Studies*, 37(6), 897–914.

Jensen, M. C. & Meckling, W. H. (1976). 'Theory of the firm: Managerial behavior, agency costs and ownership structure'. *Journal of Financial Economics*, 3(4), 305–360.

Ji, Z. (2003). *A history of modern Shanghai banking: The rise and decline of China's finance capitalism*. New York: ME Sharpe.

Kang, M. K. (2018). 'The confidence trap: Japan's past bubble and China's recent bubble'. *New Political Economy*, 23(1), 1–26.

Kerr, C., Dunlop, J. T. & Harbison, F. H. (1960). *Industrialism and industrial man: The problems of labor and management in economic growth*. Cambridge, MA: Harvard University Press.

KPMG Huazhen, (2011). *Mainland China Banking Survey*, Beijing: KPMG Huazhen.

Kwak, J. (2013). 'Cultural capture and the financial crisis'. In D. Carpenter, & D. Moss (Eds), *Preventing regulatory capture: Special interest influence and how to limit it* (pp. 71–98). Cambridge: Cambridge University Press.

Kwok, D. & Flaherty, M. (2009, April 10). 'Amex, Allianz raise $1.9 billion in ICBC stake sales'. Reuters. Retrieved from: www.reuters.com/article/us-icbc-shares/amex-allianz-raise-1-9-billion-in-icbc-stake-sales-idUSTRE53R1KW20090428.

LaMoshi, G. (2004, August 14). 'HSBC buys back into China's banking market'. *Asia Times*. Retrieved from: www.atimes.com/atimes/China/FH14Ad05.html.

Lardy, N. R. (1995). 'The role of foreign trade and investment in China's economic transformation'. *The China Quarterly*, 144, 1065–1082.

Lau, F. & Barreto, E. (2013, May 21). 'Goldman exits China's ICBC, seven years and billions later'. Reuters. Retrieved from: www.reuters.com/article/us-goldman-icbc/goldman-exits-chinas-icbc-seven-years-and-billions-later-idUSBRE94J08220130521.

Lau, L. J., Qian, Y. & Roland, G. (2000). 'Reform without losers: An interpretation of China's dual-track approach to transition'. *Journal of Political Economy*, 108(1), 120–143.

Lawrence, T. B., Leca, B. & Zilber, T. B. (2013). 'Institutional work: Current research, new directions and overlooked issues'. *Organization Studies*, 34(8), 1023–1033.

Lawrence, T., Suddaby, R. & Leca, B. (2011). 'Institutional work: Refocusing institutional studies of organization'. *Journal of Management Inquiry*, 20(1), 52–58.

Leigh, L. & Podpiera, R. (2006). *The rise of foreign investment in China's banks: Taking stock*. Washington, DC: International Monetary Fund.

Li, C. (2016). *Chinese politics in the Xi Jinping era: Reassessing collective leadership*. Washington, DC: Brookings Institution Press.

Li, F. U. (2010). 'The Financial Domination in Manchukuo'. *Journal of Foreign Studies*, 2010 (3).

Li, X. (2009). 'Ex-managers of Bank of China found guilty in US'. *China Daily*. September 2. Retrieved from: www.chinadaily.com.cn/china/2008-09/02/content_6988048.htm.

Li, X. (2009, December 13). 'Conference: Bank regulator criticizes Western counterparts', *Caijing*. Retrieved from: http://english.caijing.com.cn/2008-12-13/110038579.html.

Lin, J. Y., Cai, F. & Li, Z. (2003). *The China miracle: Development strategy and economic reform*. Beijing: Chinese University Press.

Liu, M. (2009, June 28). 'Basic rules helped China sidestep bank crisis'. *Financial Times.* Retrieved from: www.ft.com/content/63d41c2e-6411-11de-a818-00144feabdc0

Liu, Q. (2006). 'Corporate governance in China: Current practices, economic effects and institutional determinants'. *CESifo Economic Studies*, 52(2), 415–453.

Löchel, H. & Li, H. X. (2011). *Understanding the high profitability of Chinese banks* (Working Paper Series No. 177). Frankfurt: Frankfurt School of Finance & Management.

Loechel, H., Packham, N. & Li, H. X. (2010). *International banking regulation and supervision after the crisis.* (EU-China BMT Working Papers Series No. 13). Retrieved from: https://ssrn.com/abstract=1742327.

Lovell, J. (2012). *The Opium War: Drugs, dreams and the making of China*. London: Picador.

Lu, Q. (2007). *Long-term commitment, trust and the rise of foreign banking in China.* Oxford: Chandos.

Lu, Y. (2012, September 6). 'WTO China UnionPay ruling paves Way for Visa, Mastercard', China Briefing. Retrieved from: www.china-briefing.com.

Lukes, S. (1974). *Power: A radical view* (Vol. 1). London: Macmillan.

Luo, Y. (2007). *Global dimensions of corporate governance.* Oxford: Wiley-Blackwell.

Luo, Y. (2008). 'The changing Chinese culture and business behavior: The perspective of intertwinement between guanxi and corruption'. *International Business Review*, 17(2), 188–193.

Mahoney, J. & Thelen, K. (2010). 'A theory of gradual institutional change'. In J. Mahoney & K. Thelen (Eds), *Explaining institutional change: Ambiguity, agency, and power* (pp. 1–37). Cambridge: Cambridge University Press.

Man, Z. (2009, August 5). 'CBRC moves to regulate derivatives'. *Caijing*. Retrieved from: www.caijing.com.cn/2009-08-05/110220979.html.

Mander, J. (Ed.). (2014). *The case against the global economy: And for a turn towards localization*. London: Routledge.

Martin, B. (2016, November 17). 'JP Morgan fined $264m for breaching bribery laws by hiring Chinese "princelings"'. *The Telegraph*. Retrieved from www.telegraph.co.uk/business/2016/11/17/jp-morgan-fined-264m-for-breaching-bribery-laws-by-hiring-chines.

McGregor, R. (2010). *The Party: The secret world of China's communist rulers.* London: Penguin.

McSweeney, B. (2002). 'Hofstede's model of national cultural differences and their consequences: A triumph of faith-a failure of analysis'. *Human Relations*, 55(1), 89–118.

'Meet Pan Gongsheng: Get the whole story of AgBank IPO'. (2010, July 20). *Caijing*. Retrieved from: http://misc.caijing.com.cn/templates/inc/webcontentens.jsp?id=110482453&time=2010-07-20&cl=104&page=allMeet%20Pan%20Gongsheng:%20Get%20the%20Whole%20Story%20of%20AgBank%20IPO.

Meier, M., Lütkewitte, M., Mellewigt, T. & Decker, C. (2016). 'How managers can build trust in strategic alliances: A meta-analysis on the central trust-building mechanisms'. *Journal of Business Economics*, 86(3), 229–257.

Meyer, J. & Rowan, B. (1977). 'Institutionalised organizations: formal structure as myth and ceremony'. *American Journal of Sociology*, 83(2), 340–363.

Mingfu, L. (2010). *The China dream: Great power thinking and strategic posture in the post-America era.* New York: CN Times Books.

Mitchell, T. (2017, June 24). 'Contenders vie to take up mantle of Chinese central bank reforms'. *Financial Times.* Retrieved from: www.ft.com/content/f13ff49c-5725-11e7-9fed-c19e2700005f.

Mitchell, T. (2018, March 23). 'Liu He, the man in charge of China's economy'. *Financial Times*. Retrieved from: www.ft.com/content/f4f29e14-2dcb-11e8-9b4b-bc4b9f08f381.

Morgan, G., Edwards, T. & Gomes, M. V. (2014). 'Consolidating neo-institutionalism in the field of organizations: Recent contributions'. *Organization*, 21(6), 933–946.

Munir, K. A. (2015). 'A loss of power in institutional theory'. *Journal of Management Inquiry*, 24(1), 90–92.

Naughton, B. (2006). *Waves of criticism: Debates over bank sales to foreigners and neo-liberal economic policy* (China Leadership Monitor no. 17). Stanford: Hoover Institution.

Naughton, B. (2007). *The Chinese economy: Transitions and growth*. Cambridge, MA: MIT Press.

Ning, Y. & Huawei, L. (2005, October 31). 'Opposition casts doubt on Bank of China's restructuring'. *Caijing*. Retrieved from: http://english.caijing.com.cn/2005-10-31/100013962.html.

Nishimura, S. (2005). 'The foreign and native banks in China: Chop loans in Shanghai and Hankow before 1914'. *Modern Asian Studies, 39*(1), 109–132.

Nolan, J. (2009). 'Reforming the financial sector: The next step in China's development'. *Asia Pacific Business Review*, 15(4), 587–595.

Nolan, J. (2010) 'The influence of Western banks on corporate governance in China'. *Asia-Pacific Business Review* 16(3): 401–420.

Nolan, J. (2011). 'Good guanxi and bad guanxi: Western bankers and the role of network practices in institutional change in China'. *The International Journal of Human Resource Management*, 22(16), 3357–3372.

Nolan, J. (2012) 'Continuity and change in guanxi networks in East Asia: implications for the global manager'. In M. Warner (Ed.), *Managing across diverse cultures in East Asia: Issues and challenges in a changing globalized world* (pp. 168–182). London: Routledge.

Nolan, J., Rowley, C. & Warner, M. (2016). *Business networks in East Asian capitalisms: Enduring trends, emerging patterns*. Oxford: Chandos Publishing.

Nolan, P. H. (1995). *China's rise, Russia's fall: Politics, economics and planning in the transition from Stalinism*. London: Palgrave Macmillan.

Nolan, P. H. (2001). *China and the global economy: National champions, industrial policy and the big business revolution*. London: Palgrave Macmillan.

Nolan, P. H. (2004). *Transforming China: Globalization, transition and development*. London: Anthem Press.

Nolan, P. H. (2014). 'Globalisation and industrial policy: The case of China'. *The World Economy*, 37(6), 747–764.

North, D. (1981) *Structure and change in economic history*. New York: W. W. Norton.

Ortiz, D., Myers, D., Walls, E. & Diaz, M. E. (2005). 'Where do we stand with newspaper data?' *Mobilization: An International Quarterly*, 10(3), 397–419.

Palma, S. (2017, July 3). Top 1000 World Banks – 'China boosts its numbers while ICBC retains lead'. *The Banker*. Retrieved from: www.thebanker.com/Top-1000-World-Banks/Top-1000-World-Banks-China-boosts-its-numbers-while-ICBC-retains-lead.

Park, S. H. & Luo, Y. (2001). 'Guanxi and organizational dynamics: Organizational networking in Chinese firms'. *Strategic Management Journal*, 22(5), 455–477.

Paulson, H. (2015). *Dealing with China*. New York: Twelve.

Pearson, M. M. (2005). 'The business of governing business in China: Institutions and norms of the emerging regulatory state'. *World Politics*, 57(2), 296–322.

Pearson, M. M. (2007). 'Governing the Chinese economy: Regulatory reform in the service of the state'. *Public Administration Review*, 67(4), 718–730.

Pei, Y. (2010, June 22). '11 cornerstone investors chosen for AgBank IPO'. China.org.cn. Retrieved from: www.china.org.cn/business/2010-06/22/content_20321418.htm.

Peng, Y. (2007). *The Chinese banking industry: Lessons from history for today's challenges.* London: Routledge.

Peyrefitte, A. (2013). *The immobile empire.* New York: Vintage.

Pilling, D. (2017, June 13). 'Chinese investment in Africa: Beijing's testing ground'. *Financial Times.* Retrieved from: www.ft.com/content/0f534aa4-4549-11e7-8519-9f94ee97d996.

Podolny, J. M. & Page, K. L. (1998). 'Network forms of organization'. *Annual Review of Sociology*, 24(1), 57–76.

Podpiera, R. (2006). *Progress in China's banking sector reform: Has bank behaviour changed?* (IMF Working Paper WP/06/71). Washington, DC: International Monetary Fund.

Popov, V. (2000). 'Shock therapy versus gradualism: The end of the debate'. *Comparative Economic Studies*, 42(1), 1–57.

Porta, R. L., Lopez-de-Silanes, F., Shleifer, A. & Vishny, R. W. (1998). 'Law and finance'. *Journal of Political Economy*, 106(6), 1113–1155.

Preston, D. (2000). *The Boxer Rebellion: The dramatic story of China's war on foreigners that shook the world in the summer of 1900.* New York: Bloomsbury Publishing.

PriceWaterhouseCoopers. (2008). *Foreign banks in China.* Hong Kong: PricewaterhouseCoopers. Retrieved from: www.pwc.com.

PriceWaterhouseCoopers. (2014). *Future directions for foreign banks in China.* Hong Kong: PWC. Retrieved from: www.ey.com/Publication/vwLUAssets/EY-foreign-bank-china-report-2014/$FILE/EY-foreign-bank-china-report-2014.pdf.

PriceWaterhouseCoopers. (2016). *Chinese bankers survey.* Hong Kong: PWC. Retrieved from: www.pwccn.com/en/banking/chinese-banker-survey-2016.pdf.

Putnam, R. D. (1995). 'Bowling alone: America's declining social capital'. *Journal of Democracy*, 6(1), 65–78.

Ragin, C. C. (1987). *The comparative method: Moving beyond qualitative and quantitative strategies.* Berkeley: University of California Press.

Rawski, T. G. (1989). *Economic growth in prewar China.* Berkeley: University of California Press.

Rawski, T. G. (1995). 'Implications of China's Reform experience'. *The China Quarterly*, 144, 1150–1173.

Reid, A. & Yangwen, Z. (2009). *Negotiating asymmetry: China's place in Asia.* Singapore: NUS Press.

Redding, G. (2005). 'The thick description and comparison of societal systems of capitalism'. *Journal of International Business Studies*, 36(2): 123–155.

Redding, G. & Witt, M. (2007). *The future of Chinese capitalism.* Oxford: Oxford University Press.

Robinson, W. I. (2012). 'Global capitalism theory and the emergence of transnational elites'. *Critical Sociology*, 38(3), 349–363.

Rolfe, G. (2006). 'Validity, trustworthiness and rigour: quality and the idea of qualitative research'. *Journal of Advanced Nursing*, 53(3), 304–310.

Rowley, C. (2017). 'Whither globalisation and convergence? Asian examples and future research'. *Asia Pacific Business Review*, 23(1), 1–9.

Rowley, C., Benson, J. & Warner, M. (2004). 'Towards an Asian model of human resource management? A comparative analysis of China, Japan and South Korea'. *The International Journal of Human Resource Management*, 15(4–5), 917–933.

Sachs, J. & Woo, W. T. (1994). 'Structural factors in the economic reforms of China, Eastern Europe, and the former Soviet Union'. *Economic Policy*, 9(18), 101–145.

Sachs, J. & Woo, W. T. (2003). 'China's economic growth after WTO membership'. *Journal of Chinese Economic and Business Studies*, 1(1), 1–31.

Sadan, E. (1997). *Empowerment and community planning: Theory and practice of people-focused social solutions*. Tel Aviv: Hakibbutz Hameuchad Publishers.

Sandelowski, M. & Barroso, J. (2002). 'Reading qualitative studies'. *International Journal of Qualitative Methods*, 1(1), 74–108.

Schenk, C. (2001) *Hong Kong as an international financial centre: Emergence and development 1945–1965*. London: Routledge.

Schmidt, V. A. (2008). 'Discursive institutionalism: The explanatory power of ideas and discourse'. *Annual Review of Political Science*, 11(May), 303–326.

Schmidt, V. A. (2010). 'Taking ideas and discourse seriously: Explaining change through discursive institutionalism as the fourth 'new institutionalism''. *European Political Science Review*, 2(1), 1–25.

Scott, R. (2001). *Institutions and organizations*. Los Angeles: Sage.

Scott, R. (2008). *Institutions and organizations: Ideas and interests* (3rd edition). Los Angeles: Sage.

Shih, V. C. (2008). *Factions and finance in China*. Cambridge: Cambridge University Press.

Shleifer, A. & Vishny, R. W. (1997). 'A survey of corporate governance'. *The Journal of Finance*, 52(2), 737–783.

'Sleepy Giant: China Inc needs better management to become more productive'. (2016, June 23). *The Economist*. Retrieved from: www.economist.com/news/business/21701151-china-inc-needs-better-management-become-more-productive-sleepy-giant.

Smith, P. B. (2006). 'When elephants fight, the grass gets trampled: The GLOBE and Hofstede projects'. *Journal of International Business Studies*, 37(6), 915–921.

Spence, J. D. (1990). *The search for modern China*. New York: W. W. Norton & Company.

Steinmo, S. (2008). 'What is historical institutionalism?' In D. Della Porta & M. Keating (Eds), *Approaches and methodologies in the social sciences: A pluralist perspective* (pp. 118–138). Cambridge: Cambridge University Press.

Stiglitz, J. E. (2010). *Freefall: America, free markets, and the sinking of the world economy*. New York: W. W. Norton & Company.

Stiglitz, J. E. (2014). 'Transition to a market economy'. In S. Fan, R. Kanbur, S. Wei, & X. Zhang (Eds), *The Oxford companion to the economics of China* (pp. 36–41). Oxford: Oxford University Press.

Strauss, A. & Corbin, J. (1998). *Basics of qualitative research: Procedures and techniques for developing grounded theory*. London: Sage.

Suddaby, R. (2010). 'Challenges for institutional theory'. *Journal of Management Inquiry*, 19(1), 14–20.

Tang, F. & Yu, X. (2018, 26 March). 'So who's really in charge at China's central bank? New double-headed leadership muddies the waters'. *South China Morning Post*. Retrieved from: www.scmp.com/news/china/economy/article/2138979/so-whos-really-charge-chinas-central-bank-new-double-headed.

Thornberg, R. (2012). 'Informed grounded theory'. *Scandinavian Journal of Educational Research*, 56(3), 243–259.

'Too big to hail: China's banking behemoths are too beholden to the state'. (2013, August 31). *The Economist*. Retrieved from: www.economist.com/news/leaders/21584342-chinas-banking-behemoths-are-too-beholden-state-it-time-set-finance-free-too-big.

Transparency International. (2010). *Corruption Perceptions Index 2010*. Berlin: Transparency International. Retrieved from: www.transparency.org/cpi2010/results.

Triandis, H. C. (2004). 'The many dimensions of culture'. *The Academy of Management Executive*, 18(1), 88–93.

Tsai, K. S. (2007). *Capitalism without democracy: The private sector in contemporary China*. Ithacha: Cornell University Press.

Tsai, K. S. (2015) *Financing small and medium enterprises in China: Recent trends and prospects beyond shadow banking* (HKUST IEMS Working Paper No. 2015). Hong Kong: Hong Kong University of Science and Technology IEMS.

Tung, R. L. & Worm, V. (2001). 'Network capitalism: The role of human resources in penetrating the China market'. *International Journal of Human Resource Management*, 12(4), 517–534.

Urquhart, C. (2012). *Grounded theory for qualitative research: A practical guide*. London: Sage.

Vogel, E. (2011). *Deng Xiaoping and the transformation of China*. Cambridge, MA: Belknap Press of Harvard University Press.

Wade, R. (1998). 'The Asian debt-and-development crisis of 1997: Causes and consequences'. *World Development*, 26(8), 1535–1553.

Walter, C. (2014, September 26). 'The nine lives of China's central bank chief Zhou Xiaochuan'. *Forbes Asia*. Retrieved from: www.forbes.com/sites/carlwalter/2014/09/26/the-nine-lives-of-zhou-xiaochuan/#1b9bac0330c4.

Walzer, M. (1986). 'The politics of Foucault'. In D. C. Hoy (Ed.), *Foucault: A critical reader* (pp. 51–68). Oxford: Blackwell.

Wang, H. (2007). 'Linking up with the international track: What's in a slogan?' *The China Quarterly*, 189(May), 1–23.

Wang, Z. (2014). *Never forget national humiliation: Historical memory in Chinese politics and foreign relations*. New York: Columbia University Press.

Wank, D. (2002). 'Business-state clientelism in China: Decline or evolution'. In T. Gold, D. Guthrie & D. Wank (Eds), *Social connections in China: Institutions, culture, and the changing nature of guanxi* (pp. 97–116). Cambridge: Cambridge University Press.

Warner, M. (1992). *How Chinese managers learn: Management and industrial training in China*. Basingstoke: Macmillan.

Warner, M. (2010). 'In search of Confucian HRM: Theory and practice in Greater China and beyond'. *The International Journal of Human Resource Management*, 21 (12), 2053–2078.

Warner, M. (Ed.). (2013). *Managing across diverse cultures in East Asia: Issues and challenges in a changing globalized world*. London: Routledge.

Warner, M. (2014a). *Understanding management in China: Past, present and future*. London: Routledge.

Warner, M. (2014b). *Culture and management in Asia*. London: Routledge.

Warner, M. (Ed.). (2014c). *Confucian HRM in greater China: Theory and practice*. London: Routledge.

Warner, M. (2016). 'Whither "Confucian Management"?' *Frontiers of Philosophy in China*, 11(4), 608–632.

Warner, M. (Ed.) (2017). *The diffusion of Western economic ideas in East Asia.* London: Routledge.

Warner, M. & Goodall, K. (2010). *Management training and development in China: Educating managers in a globalized economy.* London: Routledge.

Watkins, H. S. & Liu, R. (1996). 'Collectivism, individualism and in-group membership: implications for consumer complaining behaviors in multicultural contexts'. *Journal of International Consumer Marketing*, 8(3–4), 69–96.

Weber, M. (1904/2011). 'Objectivity in social science and social policy'. In M. Weber, *The methodology of the social sciences* (pp. 49–112). New Jersey: Transaction Publishers.

Weber, M. (1905/2002). *The protestant ethic and the spirit of capitalism and other writings.* London: Penguin.

Weber, M. (1915/1968) *The religion of China: Confucianism and Taoism.* New York: The Free Press.

Weber, M. (1947/2009). *The theory of social and economic organization.* New York: Simon and Schuster.

Weingast, B. (2002). 'Rational-choice individualism'. In I. Katznelson & H. Milner (Eds), *Political Science: State of the Discipline* (pp. 670–692). New York: W. W. Norton & Company.

Whitley, R. (1992). *Business systems in East Asia: Firms, markets and societies,* London: Sage.

Whitley, R. (1999). *Divergent capitalisms: The social structuring and change of business systems.* Oxford: Oxford University Press.

Wildau, G. (2014, October 30). 'China to open bank cards to foreign competition'. *Financial Times.* Retrieved from: www.ft.com/content/6945f854-6027-11e4-98e6-00144feabdc0.

Wildau, G. (2015, May 31). 'China opens door for Visa and MasterCard to challenge UnionPay'. *Financial Times.* Retrieved from: www.ft.com/content/6a71b148-0764-11e5-a58f-00144feabdc0.

Wildau, G. & Lockett, H. (2017, November 10). 'China pledges to open finance section to foreign ownership'. *Financial Times.* Retrieved from: www.ft.com/content/d4a85422-c5d5-11e7-b2bb-322b2cb39656.

Williamson, O. (1981). 'The economics of organization: The transaction cost approach'. *American Journal of Sociology*, 87(3), 548–577.

Willmott, H. (2015). 'Why institutional theory cannot be critical'. *Journal of Management Inquiry*, 24(1), 105–111.

Wilson, E. (2010, April 6). 'Foreign banks' retreat prompts rethink of their China influence'. Euromoney. Retrieved from: www.euromoney.com/article/b12khzzhhtd8q0/foreign-banks-retreat-prompts-rethink-of-their-china-influence.

Wines, M. (2010, July 6). 'China Bank I.P.O. raises $19 billion'. *The New York Times.* Retrieved from: www.nytimes.com/2010/07/07/business/global/07ipo.html.

Witt, M. A. (2006). *Changing Japanese capitalism: Societal coordination and institutional adjustment.* Cambridge: Cambridge University Press.

Witt, M. A. (Ed.). (2012). *Asian business and management.* London: Sage.

Witt, M. & Redding, G. (Eds). (2013). *The Oxford handbook of Asian business systems.* Oxford: Oxford University Press.

Wong, J. (2016). *Zhu Rongji and China's economic take-off.* Singapore: World Scientific.

Wright, C. (2007, April 1). 'Why the China rainmaker just won't go away'. *Euromoney.* Retrieved from: www.euromoney.com/article/b13222lpmcv692/why-the-china-rainmaker-just-wont-go-away.

Xia, M. (2018). 'China's Financial Crisis in the Making-Soft Budget Constraint, Overdraft and the Missing Credible Commitment'. *Journal of Chinese Political Science*, 1–24.

Xin, L. (2008, December 13). 'Bank regulator criticizes Western counterparts'. *Caijing*. Retrieved from: http://english.caijing.com.cn/2008-12-13/110038579.html.

Xu, M. (2005). *Resolution of Non-performing Loans in China*. (Leonard N. Stern School of Business). New York: Glucksman Institute for Research in Securities. Retrieved from: http://w4.stern.nyu.edu/glucksman/docs/Xu_2005.pdf.

Yamagishi, T., Cook, K. S. & Watabe, M. (1998). 'Uncertainty, trust, and commitment formation in the United States and Japan'. *American Journal of Sociology, 104*(1), 165–194.

Yan, H. & Huang, Y. (2008). 'Deposit insurance and banking supervision in China: The agenda ahead'. *The Geneva Papers on Risk and Insurance-Issues and Practice*, 33(3), 547–565.

Yang, B. (1997). *Deng: A political biography*. New York: ME Sharpe.

Yang, D. L. (1996). *Calamity and reform in China: State, rural society, and institutional change since the Great Leap Famine*. Palo Alto, CA: Stanford University Press.

Yang, M. M. H. (1994). *Gifts, favors, and banquets: The art of social relationships in China*. Ithaca, NY: Cornell University Press.

Yang, M. M. H. (2002). 'The resilience of guanxi and its new deployments: A critique of some new guanxi scholarship'. *The China Quarterly*, 170, 459–476.

Yao, K. & Zhang, S. (2018, March 25). 'China's new central bank chief pledges steady opening of financial sector'. Reuters. Retrieved from: www.reuters.com/article/us-china-economy-cenbank/chinas-new-central-bank-chief-pledges-steady-opening-of-financial-sector-idUSKBN1H106N.

Young, K. (2013). 'Policy takers or policy makers? The lobbying of global banking regulators'. *Business Horizons*, 56(6), 691–701.

Yu, F. (2017, February 26). '"Princeling" hirings complicate business in China for global banks'. *Epoch Times*. Retrieved from: www.theepochtimes.com/princeling-hires-complicate-global-banks-operations-in-china_2227066.html.

Zhai, Y. (2017). 'Traditional values and political trust in China'. *Journal of Asian and African Studies*. 53(3), 350–365.

Zhang, J. (2017). 'Western ideas of corporate governance: China's reform of large state-owned enterprises'. In M. Warner (Ed.). *The diffusion of Western economic ideas in East Asia* (pp. 360–373). London: Routledge.

Zhang, W. & Ke, R. (2003, June). *Trust in China: A cross-regional analysis*. (William Davidson Institute Working Paper No. 586). Ann Arbour: William Davidson Institute. Retrieved from: http://dx.doi.org/10.2139/ssrn.577781.

Zhao, S. (1997). 'Chinese intellectuals' quest for national greatness and nationalistic writing in the 1990s'. *The China Quarterly*, 152, 725–745.

Zhen, Y. (2009, February 19). 'Audit uncovers 6b yuan in financial fraud', *China Daily*. Retrieved from: www.chinadaily.com.cn/business/2009-02/19/content_7492849.htm.

Zhou, L. (2009, February 27). 'In China, speculators need to pay to play'. *Caijing*. Retrieved from: http://english.caijing.com.cn/2009-02-27/110075072.html.

Zhu, Y., Warner, M. & Rowley, C. (2007). 'Human resource management with "Asian" characteristics: A hybrid people-management system in East Asia'. *The International Journal of Human Resource Management*, 18(5), 745–768.

Index

For Product Safety Concerns and Information please contact our EU representative GPSR@taylorandfrancis.com
Taylor & Francis Verlag GmbH, Kaufingerstraße 24, 80331 München, Germany

www.ingramcontent.com/pod-product-compliance
Ingram Content Group UK Ltd.
Pitfield, Milton Keynes, MK11 3LW, UK
UKHW011018180926
475701UK00004B/813

* 9 7 8 0 3 6 7 5 8 5 2 1 1 *